D1321831

The Days of the Years
of My Pilgrimage

The Days of the Years of My Pilgrimage

G. N. M. Collins

KNOX PRESS [EDINBURGH]

THE KNOX PRESS [EDINBURGH]
15 North Bank Street, Edinburgh EH1 2LS

© Trustees of the late G. N. M. Collins

First published 1991

Typeset by Action Typesetting Ltd, Gloucester
Printed and bound in Great Britain by
Billing & Sons Ltd, Worcester

CONTENTS

ILLUSTRATIONS

1. A view of the Sutherland Hills

2. Dr. Collins' grandmother

3. Mr Duncan MacRae

4. Interior of the Gaelic Free Church, Greenock

5. Moderator of the General Assembly, 1949

6. Free St. Columba's Church
    (By courtesy of George Thomson, LRPS)

7. Interior of St. Columba's
    (By courtesy of George Thomson, LRPS)

8. At the Reformed Ecumenical Synod

9. Dr. Collins with his wife

10. The Free Church College
    (By courtesy of George Thomson, LRPS)

11. With the Queen at the General Assembly, 1977
    (By courtesy of Scotsman Publications)

12. At the BBC special luncheon, 1988
    (By courtesy of the BBC)

Illustrations appear between pages 72 and 73

ACKNOWLEDGMENTS

I wish to explain my involvement with this book and to acknowledge those who, in various ways, have contributed far more to its appearance than I have myself.

We are all indebted to a close friend of Dr. Collins from whom I learned, only months before his death as it turned out, that this autobiographical material existed.

My offer to have it put on Word Processor disks and do the preliminary editorial work was accepted by Dr. Collins with much modesty and yet with great courtesy. Feeling, even then, that our time was short, I am grateful to my younger daughter, Mhairi, for her interest and for the hours she devoted to the typing, and re-typing, of the material at that stage.

Once on disk, corrections and print-outs were easy and, happily, enabled Dr. Collins to bring his own editorial experience and skills to the final draft. Providentially, his work on the last three chapters was almost complete when he suffered the stroke which hospitalised him for the remaining weeks of his life.

I wish to set on record the personal pleasure it afforded me to work with him in the closing days of his pilgrimage. The hours spent in this way were to my own profit.

Special thanks are due to Miss Rene Stewart and Miss Mairi MacPherson for invaluable help and advice during that period; to the Trustees of his estate for a generous grant towards production costs; and, finally, to the Rev John J. Murray of the Knox Press [Edinburgh] for the considerable task of seeing the work through the press, and to the latter for undertaking its actual publication.

J. Douglas Macmillan.
Edinburgh, January 1991.

Biographical Introduction

J. Douglas MacMillan

Sadness and gratitude were strangely mingled at the news of the homecall of the Rev. Dr. George N. M. Collins, Edinburgh, on the 20th October 1989.There was sadness because his going had that quality of epochal significance we commonly associate only with men whose ministries, under God, so firmly mould the character of the Church for good that their death seems to spell the end of an era: there was gratitude for a life spent in the service of Christ and grown so rich in years and grace that none could begrudge his being taken, nor feel that it involved anything other than the perfect crown and complement of saving faith – the reward of being "with Christ, which is far better."

Widely known throughout the Christian world, George Norman MacLeod Collins was a minister of the Free Church of Scotland and Professor Emeritus of the Free Church College, Edinburgh. Ordained to his first Pastorate in the Free Gaelic Church, Greenock, as far back as June 1928, his sixty-one years of ministry were to prove as unique in their quiet influence as they were in length. Throughout that time, he was a faithful witness to the Master he loved and a splendid ambassador of the Church through which he served Him, and in which he had been, of late, the most senior man in the ministry.

It was this loyal attachment to her witness which made his name virtually synonymous with the life of the Free Church through the years, not only in the minds of those within her own borders but also by the wider Christian community. But although all who knew him felt how deeply he loved his own Church and saw how well he served her, it was equally clear that, like his great Free Church predecessor – and to some extent, one thinks, his model – of last century, Thomas Chalmers, his mind and heart had such a generous interest in the wider welfare of the Gospel that, ultimately, he belonged to, and worked for the good of, "all that in every place call upon the name of Jesus Christ our Lord".

Professor Collins had a unique background. Born one of a family of four in the London of 1901, his father was a Londoner and his mother a Highlander who had left her Sutherland home to work in

London when she was only fourteen. In 1909, an uncle took the small George up to his maternal grandmother, Mrs Dolina MacLeod, Elphin, for the summer to recuperate from some childhood illness. This single step in providence was to have an unforeseen influence upon his entire life and future.

He used to tell how, on his first morning there his uncle made him a fishing rod and took him up the burnside to catch his first fish. His aunt introduced him to scones and oatcakes baked over a peat fire, and his grandmother taught him, patiently and lovingly, to speak Gaelic. At the end of the summer he declined to go home, and was enrolled in the local school. It was not the great city but the Highland village that was to mould the growing lad and, among other things, it contributed two ingredients that were to inform his life-calling, determine the directions of his ministry, and focus its areas of influence.

First, it placed him in an environment where Gaelic was still the everyday language of home and playground and gave him such a love for the ancient tongue as, in later years, made him master of a fluid, idiomatic, Gaelic style which he could exploit to great advantage and that equipped him to serve his Master and his Church not only in the Lowland areas, where he actually ministered in two bilingual congregations, but throughout the Highlands and Islands. His fine Gaelic preaching was one factor, among others, that won him a warmly-attached following from amongst Gaelic-speaking believers in those areas which few of his peers could rival and none of them could surpass.

But the second feature of this providence is more important yet, for his upbringing also brought him under the influence of a godly home and of a discerning circle of Christian people. They were of the number whose faith had only recently come through the testing fires of the ecclesiastical upheaval of 1900 and its effects upon Free Church people in the Scotland of that time. Brought up in a spiritual atmosphere where the things that matter most were crisply and explicitly held and defined, the growing boy came to appreciate the importance of sound doctrine to practical Christianity and to see that a knowledge of past events in the Church of God is essential to a right appreciation of her current circumstances at any one time.

Perhaps the greatest spiritual influence in those formative years was that of Duncan MacRae, elder of the Free Church in Elphin. This saintly man liked to write many letters to a wide circle of Christian friends, but he had a withered hand and needed a secretary. George became his willing right hand and in doing so read and wrote much that puzzled him: like the godly women of Bunyan's *Grace Abounding*, the content of the correspondence was deeply spiritual, and the young secretary realised that those folk possessed a delightful secret that he did not understand. Duncan MacRae never would preach but preferred to read a sermon by one of the divines — Owen, or Spurgeon, or Robert Murray M'Cheyne. And the Holy Spirit worked in the young hearer's heart.

In spite of urgings and promptings from Duncan MacRae and others — or, perhaps because of them — he refused to consider the possibility that he should enter the ministry and returned to London in his late teens to study journalism. Although he enjoyed this immensely it seems that the question of the ministry grew upon him until, at length, he had to yield.

This led back to Scotland and to a theological course in the Free Church College, Edinburgh, undertaken concurrently with studies for the external B.A. of London University; these courses were completed in 1927 and 1928 respectively. In 1927 he was invited by the Church to initiate the founding of a Free Church work in Toronto and he gave himself heartily to this until returning to begin his ministry in the Gaelic Free Church, Greenock, in June 1928. He was to be in Toronto again through 1930 – 31 for a year of ministry and study during which he completed his B.D. at Toronto University (after completing 1st and 2nd year exams with Glasgow), graduating with distinction in Systematic Theology and Church History in 1932. After ten years in his Greenock charge, he was called, in 1938, to succeed Dr Alexander Stewart in Free St Columba's, Edinburgh, then as now, one of the most prominent and significant pulpits in the Free Church.

It was in this pulpit — made famous by the redoubtable Thomas Guthrie — that his reputation was secured as a gifted and lucid preacher and from it he exercised an influential, evangelical, expository, and soundly biblical ministry for twenty-five years. His preaching and pastoral work were, with God's blessing, effective amongst young and old and successive generations of the Church's ministry, as well as other University and College students, were moulded by his clear, spiritual, teaching. In this way, he became well-known and deeply-respected throughout his own Church and won the place of personal friend and wise counsellor to many of her ministers. His sphere of influence, while changing its base, was extended and all the more clearly confirmed by his appointment, on the retiral of Dr. A. M. Renwick, to the Chair of Church History in the Free Church College in May 1963. From this post he formally retired in 1982, although continuing to teach some classes until the end of Session 1983.

His influence as a minister was also enhanced, and its usefulness greatly augmented, through his work as Editor of the Church's magazines over a very long period — *The Instructor* from 1937 – 58, and *The Monthly Record* from 1958 – 73 — and this was another area in which it reached far beyond the frontiers of his own denomination. Also, through the years his journalistic urges found fulfilment in the writing and the publication of a number of useful works in Christian biography and Church history. His pen sketched lively portraits of godly men who had achieved great things in their own day and so, by his writings, he extended their particular influence within the Church of God right through to this century. His appreciation of the value of Church history also prompted him to provide succinct works for the youth of today and *The Heritage of Our Fathers* — possibly his best known book and published in 1974 — is particularly valuable in its discerning account of the events which produced the present Free Church of Scotland.

Professor Collins played a leading part in the administrative work of the Church and, at various times, was Convener of important Committees such as Training of the Ministry, Public Questions, and Welfare of Youth. He was a ready speaker and shrewd debater in the General Assembly and, as Convener of the Business Committee, had the honour and privilege of receiving the Queen when she visited the Assembly in the Silver Jubilee Year. He had the unusual distinction of being twice Moderator of the General Assembly, first in 1949 and again in 1971. This was a clear indicator, not only of his personal capability but also, and perhaps particularly, a sign of the great and tender esteem in which he was held by the whole Church.

He gave valuable support to many worthy causes outwith his own denomination, among them the National Bible Society of Scotland which, for a number of years, benefited from his excellent gifts as Chairman. He was one of the first ministers in Scotland to participate in Gaelic Religious broadcasting and for close on half a century he served as member and Chairman of various B.B.C. committees involved with Gaelic Radio worship services. In November 1988 the B.B.C. marked his fine contribution to this work at a special luncheon given in his honour in Glasgow.

His genuine interest in promoting and strengthening the Reformed Churches in other lands also involved him in a lot of work but here, as in everything else to which he put his hand, his time and energies were given ungrudgingly and unstintingly. He was the driving force in the formation of the Reformed Ecumenical Synod and was responsible for organising its first meeting in 1953. This actually took place in Edinburgh and he was unanimously elected the Synod's first Moderator, an honour which was repeated in Grand Rapids ten years later. In 1984, he was honoured with the Degree of Doctor of Divinity.

He was also deeply involved, with the late Rev. Murdoch MacRae, Kinloch, in the setting up of the British Evangelical Council, and for a number of years represented the Free Church of Scotland on the Executive Committee of that body. That was a position that opened up avenues by which he could help and strengthen the hands of ministerial brethren in other parts of the United Kingdom and, amongst others, his long-lasting friendship with its minister meant that the pulpit of Westminster Chapel was one of those from which he preached at regular intervals.

These are but some of the causes through which he helped the wider Church of his Master but the one which probably took special place with him was almost certainly the Scottish Reformation Society which he served as Chairman for a long time. In many ways that Society reflected much that was dear to his heart, and the climatic event of the great Reformation which it existed to commemorate took a central place in his writing and teaching for more than fifty years.

His knowledge of seventeenth century Scotland was, in the writer's estimation, probably unrivalled in the present day and so historians of note in Britain and from overseas frequently sought his counsel and advice when working in this area of Scottish Church History. Much of his writing has brought the Church's leaders, as well as her contendings and conflicts, back out of the mists of those long-gone years and presented them to us with a wonderful freshness. One of his final books, *Men of the Burning Heart*, published in 1983, is both a model of its type and a fine illustration of how interestingly and informatively he could use his pen to feed the heart as well as the mind.

In his Master's service he travelled widely and his home became a gallery as pictures and mementos of numerous Christian events in which he took a leading part adorned the walls and shelves. His wife, Louisa Anderson, who predeceased him in January 1987, was a true helpmeet to him through their many years together and, although he never complained, it was quite clear that he felt her loss very keenly. Mrs Collins was brought up in Golspie but was from a family whose roots went back into the beautiful Strath of Halladale in the more northern part of Sutherland.

Over the two or three months of the increasing infirmity that led into his last illness he remained keenly interested in the well-being of Christ's cause and was deeply immersed in the work of preparing his memoirs. He was urged to do this by friends and it is good that he was able to complete the writing before his death.

Having become a father figure in the latter years he will be missed from the Scottish Church scene. However, from the witness he maintained right through to his dying hour we take courage, and it is our prayer that God would now be pleased to touch many of Scotland's sons with the same constraining love which motivated this, our friend, and that all of us who came under his influence might emulate the simplicity and humility which adorned his profession and commended his faith.

1: My Home from Home

In my line of vision as I write is a chipped white beaker bearing the date 29th August, 1909 and an oval picture of the young Marquis of Stafford. Such value as that tawdry ornament has for me is obviously sentimental, and the explanation of its prominence in my present surroundings is due to the fact that it marks my *annus mirabilis* − the year in which I exchanged the monstrous urbanism of London for the simple rusticity of Sutherland, the county of my maternal forbears. Needless to say, the affairs of the Marquisate of Stafford had nothing to do with my change of residence, but it just so happened that the Marquis, who was heir to the Dukedom of Sutherland, had come of age on August 29th, 1909, and that I, who had arrived in Sutherland just a few weeks before, had been included among the thousands of school children on the Sutherland Estates who were called upon to celebrate the event. So, I found myself joining in the bumper picnics by which the auspicious occasion was registered in the minds of the juvenile residents within the young nobleman's Scottish inheritance which, in those days, was almost co-extensive with the county of Sutherland.

So if 1909 was his great year it was mine also, though for very different reasons. But the chipped beaker is still a memento of a great occasion.

The story which lay behind my coming to Scotland can be very briefly told. An illness necessitated my being out of school for a time; and, to complete my recovery, I was sent to my mother's old home in Sutherland, in care of my Uncle George, who had called on us in London on his way home from South Africa. The period of my convalescence was set at around six weeks, but even at the end of six years I was still there, and not likely to return to London.

Was it any wonder? What had London to offer that could not be outmatched by that little township of Elphin? What could England exhibit, of all its grandeur, that could compare with this rugged outback? Mountains that wrapped their hoary heads in matching folds of cloud as if in awe of their glorious Creator! Steep valleys that stored the brown waters of the singing burns. Scarred cliffs whose secrets were constantly being pried into by inquisitive geologists from all over the world! An exciting wild-life that never failed to hold the interest of the man conscious of his kinship with nature! Hills covered with verdure almost to their limestone summits, with never a warning to the stroller to "Keep off the grass!".

Many years later I recalled those early impressions of the county of my adoption during a visit to Argyllshire. Again it was a glorious day in late summer, and I was standing at a beauty-spot on the ascent from Ballachulish eastwards by the side of Loch Leven, looking down on the sparkling sea and across the loch to the hills of Lochaber, when a man who had been standing a little further up came across to speak to me.

"Sir," he began, "will you please oblige me?" "In what way?," I cannily replied. "Will you give me a good, hard pinch so as to convince me that I am really seeing all this and not just dreaming it?"

Yes, there were times when I felt just like that in my early days in Sutherland. And in like circumstances, I still do. Lord Byron was never my favourite poet, yet I feel a certain affinity with him. For had he not also been born in London, and had he not also removed to Scotland in early life to make his home there and sing the praises of the land of his adoption?

England! thy beauties are tame and domestic
To one who has roved o'er the mountains afar;
Oh for the crags that are wild and majestic,
The steep frowning glories of dark Lochnagar.

Mountainous countries have their changing moods of course, and life there is by no means a continuous blissful serenity. But even when our guardian mountains intercepted the speeding clouds and sent their contents pouring tumultuously upon us, the elements paid us for their sport and brought hordes of venturesome brown trout, of the very best quality, up into our burns and rivers for us to catch. So, who complained of the flooding? Well, we didn't; but then, we were young; and, equipped with our fishing rods, mostly home-made, we boys set out for the swollen streams and proved what enthusiasm could achieve, even with crude equipment.

Isaac Walton indeed! We could teach *The Compleat Angler* a few things!

I shall never forget my introduction to school-life in Elphin. The set-up was entirely different from what I was used to. You knew all the pupils, and in all probability were related to most of them. The pack-drill of London school-life was almost unknown in Elphin.

There were upwards of 30 pupils enrolled in the central school, and there were three "side-schools", each taught by an uncertificated teacher under the supervision of the teacher in the central school, who was fully qualified in his profession. In addition, there was a sewing-mistress for the girls, but her duties were limited to one class per week. It may be suspected that her visits were more welcome to the boys than to the girls, however; for, when the weather suited, we were taken out to the school-house garden and given some instruction in the art of Adam. At least, that was the idea; but, as it happened, none of the teachers in my time had much interest in the subject, nor did they spend much time with us, but left us almost entirely to our own devices; and few of these had any relation to gardening!

Colin MacDonald, in his *Echoes of the Glen*, describes himself and his fellow-pupils in the rather similar Ross-shire school which he attended, as "poor, unwilling sacrifices on the altar of the Moloch of learning." There were so many other and more interesting things to do. "In the city," he continues, "it is not so bad; from drab street to drabber class-room is merely a matter of degree of misery. But in the country. . .! To have to file in to that depressing atmosphere of square-roots, G.C.M's, and 'goes into's', when the sun is shining gloriously and out-of-doors allurements are strong. . .!"

Yes, I knew the feeling!

Kenneth Matheson from Ullapool was my first teacher in Elphin, but I was not long under his tuition, and I remember him only dimly as an agreeable young man who did his best with the material assigned him.

Duncan MacKenzie from Stoer followed him, but served only as a stop-gap. He had the reputation of being a knowledgeable man and a competent teacher, but for some reason or other that I never discovered, he had to be content with the mere pickings of his profession. He could fly off the handle on the slightest provocation and, knowing this, like King Agag in the Bible story, we "walked delicately" when he was around.

Sometimes, when the teacher was away for the day at one of the side-schools we had Mr. Fiddes, the United Free missionary, as his stand-in. What teaching qualification, if any, he possessed we never knew, nor were we much interested. What we *did* know was that he had been a missionary-teacher in St. Kilda for some time, and that he had some capital stories about life there, and could easily be prompted to tell them. So we always saw to it that there would be no lack of prompting, and his visits were always welcome.

Alexander MacKenzie, who was my teacher for the rest of my school-days in Elphin, was the one of my early instructors who impressed me most. A native of the place, he had all the disadvantages of "a prophet in his own country", but he overcame them well. As an educationist he was well worthy of greater advancement in his profession than ever came to him, and several of the pupils who passed through his hands made their mark in their chosen vocations.

The *cameraderie* in the playground was good, but our sports and physical exercises were not of great variety. In the excitement of living in a mountainous area I developed a modest love of climbing and, with a cousin, Roddy Campbell from Edinburgh, who was killed in the 1914-18 war, I acquired a reputation for fool-hardiness, because we had once climbed up the rock-face of the Cnoc Breac to explore a jackdaw's nest that was built on one of its highest ivy-covered ledges. For our exploit, which we had not regarded as dangerous, we were severely lectured by good Donald Macleod, the father of Roderick Macleod, the well-known Gaelic tenor, and a pioneer in the field of gramophone-record production. Donald had been watching us with growing concern, unable to reach us and afraid to shout a warning lest we should lose our concentration and hold. But his severity evoked no resentment, for the kindly care of the good man's heart shone clearly through. But my zeal for climbing suffered a set-back from which it never fully recovered!

Football we loved, and we played it by our own rules. Our favourite pitch, as it happened, was usable only in the drought of summer and the frost of winter. It was so marshy at most other times that, as an alternative, we had to make shift with a piece of land which surrounded an old school across the road. The fact that the game had to be played over a high ridge at mid-field added to the fun, for the goal at one end of the pitch could not be seen from the other. Obviously, the normal rules were not operative, and adaptations became necessary. And everything was done in dead seriousness. A referee was desirable, but not indispensable!

Our winter sports were equally adaptable. The extensive bog-land around the school meant that in the prevalent frosty weather there was no lack of ice-rinks. Skates we had none; but our strong winter boots, replete with iron toe-plates, heel-plates, tackets and sparables, served our purpose admirably. Some of us had toboggans, home-made of course, and primitive, but offering all kinds of thrills and spills when the snow became frozen over.

It may seem strange to say that our isolation was not often a serious inconvenience when our roads became snow-blocked, for we were seldom taken unawares, or unprepared. Nothing was left to chance. Each home had its own store of provisions against such emergencies — a barrel of the finest flour, a meal-chest packed with the oat-meal of Caithness or Ross-shire; a firkin or two of salt herring from Ullapool; a barrel of salted mutton from our own flocks, for this was good sheep-country; a stock of potatoes from our own fields; and if you can procure a better potato than a Champion or a Golden Wonder, a fortune awaits you! And (but tell it not in Gath, publish it not in the streets of Askelon!) there might be, there just might be, in one of the outhouses, a barrel of salted venison; but how it got there, well who could tell? So when the less-isolated townships, with their shops and delivery-vans frantically sought ways of replenishing their stores and succouring their beleaguered customers, we thankfully drew upon our reserves and waited for the weather to change.

The sheep had the worst of it, for they, largely, had to fend for themselves. Sometimes, they became buried in the snowdrifts, and when the storm came in the lambing season, as it often did, the crofters spent toilsome days searching for, and rescuing their flocks. But times of hardship seldom found them unprepared.

The care of the domestic animals was always an acceptable task to a boy who was never fully happy about animals confined in Zoological Gardens or held in virtual captivity in an environment that was foreign to their nature. Much better see them in more congenial surroundings enjoying, as far as possible, a manner of life more suited to them. On the domestic side, the shaggy croft ponies were my favourites. When *Star*, our white pony, was commandeered for national service in the 1914-18 war I made a personal declaration of war on the Kaiser who had deprived me of my most prized pet, yet felt a deep-seated satisfaction that somehow, somewhere, in his own stolid way, *Star* was making his contribution to Britain's war effort and the overthrow of tyranny. After *Star*'s departure, we acquired a spirited young mare which, in due time, presented us with a foal with which I could do almost anything.

In the final reckoning, the cows were the croft-beasts to which we owed most in the round of the year, with the sheep an easy second: but reason as you might, my supreme affection was for the croft pony. The day that I rode it to the 'smiddy' in Ullapool to be shod for the spring work was one of my annual red-letter days.

Of the wild mountain-fauna we saw but little. They had no business with humans and kept well out of their way. Stags and hinds you seldom saw except in the dead of winter when hunger might embolden them to venture down from the heights to see if there was anything to eat on the lower levels. Foxes might be there, but you did not see them because they had already seen you and had no desire to know you better. But if you were interested in the study of wild life, and had the patience that is requisite to that interest there were always rich recompenses. It is a confession of indolence for me to admit that not a great deal of that wealth came my way! The rivers and lochans were tempting and rewarding and a brown trout was always nice for tea.

From my early days I was a voracious reader. After all, there was little else one could do to pass the long winter evenings. The school library had its attractions, but its range of literature was not extensive. I was recently told that the old lending catalogue still survives and shows that I read the whole stock – some of them indeed several times over. I well remember being in such dire need of something to read that I even borrowed a book bearing the forbidding title *The Wife to Get*. I forget the author and the impression made on me by his marriage-guidance counsel. Certainly my choice of reading did not arise on that occasion from any precocious interest in matrimony, but rather from the fact that I had come to the very last of my reading resources, and, in my straits, was ready for anything.

In addition to the school library there was of course the public library, provided by Andrew Carnegie. The library became the social centre of the community — a veritable local parliament where we read the newspapers and discussed their more stirring contents, with a zeal that far outstripped our knowledge. But, no matter; it passed the evening.

It goes without saying that we were all, or nearly all, Liberals in politics! What else was there? Socialism we equated pretty much with Communism. And the Conservatives had not, even yet, lived down the odium of the land clearances. Everyone who was suspected of supporting a Tory candidate lost caste among us.

Add to all this that David Lloyd George was the bright star in the Liberal firmament at the time and you have the ultimate reason for voting Liberal. Lloyd George was a man of the people; a champion of the poor! The passing of his Old Age Pension Act in 1909 brought him national fame.

Some of the pensioners were uneasy, however. Where would all that money come from? Was it right that some people should be taxed for the benefit of others for whom they had no obligation and with whom they had no kinship? And was there not a suspicion of poor relief about it all? There was nothing they dreaded more than that they should incur the stigma , as they deemed it, of pauperism. Time and again the exciseman had to come from Ullapool to assure some of the people who were of pension age that there was nothing degrading about accepting the State-provided benefit that had been made available. But it took a time for the lesson to sink in. After all, what did they lack? In the Lord's Prayer they were taught to appeal, not for luxuries, but for "daily bread". And having "food and raiment", therewith to be content. And as for the "social service" that men were talking about, they had it already, but called it *nabaidheachd* — (neighbourliness). The Church also took a hand in the provision and distribution of this bounty when unforeseen hardship arose. There was nothing to fear! *"Jehovah jireh! The Lord will provide."*

It did not readily occur to these good people that this new form of social service was really needed, and could be the quintessence of practical Christianity. So they took their time to learn more fully about it.

Colin MacDonald of the Land Court knew the Elphin and Knockan of those years as I had known them and had sensed the contentment that was known there and throughout all the Highland area in those times, and this is how he wrote of it in his *Highland Journey*.

"If you look at a map of the Highlands you see in the gusset of Sutherland that stabs into Ross-shire the names 'Elphin and Cnocan'. In the common phrase of the unthinking these hamlets are 'miles from anywhere' — implying a superior status for the 'anywheres', and a corresponding insignificance for the places so far from them. In reality, of course, it is the other way about. For in the things that really matter, it is the 'Elphins and Cnocans' of the world that are to be congratulated and envied, and the 'anywheres' that are to be commiserated; the poor cities with their glare and their shams and their shames."

But "the old order changeth"and we change with it, glad at least that we were privileged to sample the old.

2: Breaking the Language Barrier

Elphin in the early years of this century was indeed a delightful place for a young Londoner. You soon got to know everybody, and you discovered that many of them were related to you by one degree or other of the cousinhood that survived in the Highlands even subsequent to the breakdown of the clan system after Culloden. *Cinneadas* (kinship) and *cleamhnas* (clannishness) were still of much account. But there were problems. My *Sassunach* accent, for instance, was so pronounced that I was not easily understood by my school-mates, so I decided that it must be discarded as soon as possible, and the local accent adopted in its place.

With the older people my problem of communication was quite different. They, for the most part, spoke Gaelic, and I had none. In this case the obvious solution of the difficulty was that I should acquire a working knowledge of the native tongue and thereby qualify for full citizenship in the land of my adoption. But there were no Gaelic classes, and no help could be expected from the locals in the playground, for in those days parents tended to discourage their children from using Gaelic while playing together, the assumption being that the use of Gaelic would hinder their progress in English. They *knew* the language but disdained the use of it as a medium of communication. The story was told of an Assynt lassie from a Gaelic-speaking home who went to Edinburgh to take a course in domestic science. When she returned home on holiday the following year she chanced to meet an old shepherd who greeted her effusively in Gaelic. She replied in English.

"An e gun do chaill thu a'Ghaidhlig?" (Is it that you have lost the Gaelic) exclaimed the shepherd.

Again the answer was in English; "O no, I can understand it, but cannot speak it." The retort was devastating.

"Mo thruaigh mise; an e sin a tha foghlum a'bhaile mhoir a'deanamh ort? a'toirt uat, 's chan ann a'toirt dhuit. Chan fhearr thu a nis na mo chu- chaorach. 'S ann sa'Ghaidhlig a bhitheas mi bruidhinn ris, agus tuigidh e mi, ach chan urrain e mo fhreagairt ach le comhart. Ach tha leithsgeul dha- san: cha robh e riamh ann a'chollaisd!" ("Pity me! Is that what the education of the city is doing to you: taking from you instead of giving to you! You are no

better than my sheep-dog. It is in Gaelic that I speak to him and he understands me, yet cannot answer me but with a bark. But he is to be excused; he was never in College!'").

That then was the situation when I began to learn Gaelic. It was not taught in school, nor were there classes elsewhere. Other educational facilities had to be devised; indeed, they already existed – the Church!

So much was Gaelic the *lingua franca* of the community in those days that all the Church services were conducted in that tongue, except that at the annual Communion services there was usually a short word, *"Anns a'chanan eile"*, (in the other language) as we said. And on Sabbath morning, proceeding concurrently in the nearby Reading Room, there would be an English service for the few whose early education had been so defective that they were sent out to the world with no knowledge of what we were told had been the language spoken in the Garden of Eden in better days! There might also be a kind of English epilogue to the Harvest Thanksgiving service, but only after the congregation had been scanned and an on-the-spot decision come to as to whether such a thing was really necessary.

The fact that my spiritual needs pressed upon me with less urgency than did my desire for a working knowledge of Gaelic led me into an easy concurrence with these arrangements. Painstakingly, I followed the Gaelic Scripture readings with my English Bible, noting carefully the words that I thought I understood, and listing those that made no sense to me, to be checked later with *MacLeod and Dewar's Gaelic Dictionary* – a prize won by my aunt Lexy at school, and very willingly passed on to me.

To build up a Gaelic vocabulary was one thing, however; to use it effectively was quite another, and no tutors were available. So, in my extremity, I turned to my grandmother to hear me out as I read again the Bible passages that I had been trying so hard to follow in Church and at family worship. It was a profitable exercise for me, but a testing one for my patient and devout mentor; for my reading was plentifully interspersed with mirth-provoking howlers. Withdrawing the Bible from my hand one afternoon, and with a muted laugh that even she could not fully suppress, she remarked, "We must not be laughing over the Bible, a *ghraidh*; let us take another book, and it won't matter."

The substitute book turned out to be Dr. Norman Macleod's *Caraid nan Gaidheal* – an excellent Gaelic reader over which pupil and guide could join in merriment at the beginner's mistakes without fear of being judged irreverent.

It was to my advantage that the books in my new home were nearly all religious in character, and mostly all in Gaelic, for this meant that my early reading was conditioning the tone of my spiritual life while at the same time it advanced my knowledge of the language. Of all the Gaelic religious poets my grandmother's firm favourite was Dugald Buchanan. From her facility for quoting him I should imagine that she had all his poems by heart. The time came, although not yet awhile, when I too could thrill to the rich and startling imagery of Buchanan, sense the glow of Patrick Grant's appeal and appreciate the experimental theology of John MacDonald, especially in his *An Criosduidh air a Thurus gu Iordan* (The Christian on his Way to Jordan). Since those days I have often wondered what my loss might have been had those three books been missing from our one-shelf library. They helped to teach me Gaelic, and a lot more.

Incongruously, Rob Donn's Poems found a place on that shelf, perhaps because he was a Sutherland man. But I cannot recall ever having seen the book in use until I, in a moment of literary famine, took it down and began to cast my eyes over it. It caught on. There was vulgarity, there was scurrility, there was vindictive severity, for Rob was the king of the Gaelic satirists. But withal there was a sense of moral earnestness that could not be silent in the presence of injustice and hypocrisy, and above and beyond all, in my quite immature estimation, there was a wealth of Gaelic vocabulary and a skill of phrase construction that I found quite fascinating. I followed him slowly and limpingly. Often, I lost him altogether. I, indeed, estimated his greatness by my inability to comprehend him. I probably felt about him as the Glasgow woman did who was always extolling her favourite preacher, Thomas Chalmers.

"But do you really understand him?" asked a lady who had listened to one of her eulogies. The coming rebuke signalised itself first in a baleful stare. "Understaun him!" she echoed, "Wumman, I wadna presume!"

But I retained my sense of indebtedness to Rob Donn, and was glad when years later, I read Dr. Donald Maclean's defence of him in his *The Literature of the Scottish Gael*. When Rob visited the parish of Farr his custom was to stay at the manse of Rev. George Munro, and there he engaged in prayer alternately with his host at family prayers. "Rob must not only have conducted himself with propriety," writes Dr. Maclean, "but was also looked upon as a pious man, at any rate in his latter days, otherwise the godly Mr Munro would never have asked him to lead the devotions at the family altar."

And when, as a young minister, I gave my first lecture in Gaelic to a Highland Literary Society in Greenock, the subject of my choice was *Beatha agus Bardachd Rob Dhuinn* (The Life and Poems of Rob Donn).

I owed it to him.

3: Life on the Croft

My first impression of crofting life was that, in a world essentially imperfect, it left little to be desired. True, the work was not lucrative, but it always seemed to provide what the *Shorter Catechism* describes as "a competent portion of the good things of this life". We never went hungry. What appeared on our tables was usually the yield of our own fields, the produce of our own stalls, and the honest returns of our own poultry for the adequate board and lodgings that we supplied them.

Our one and only shop consisted of a lean-to shack in Knockan where eatables were in short supply and limited variety. We did not eat shop-bread anyway. It was expensive to buy and difficult to keep fresh. We enjoyed it when we had it, but never missed it when we didn't. It was an *annas* — a rarity — on our table, and to be used sparingly. The bread produced by our ovens, as we were always being told, was better for us. Girdle-scones and brandered oat-cakes were the staple of our table, but oven-scones and ginger-bread were in frequent supply. The hanging-oven and girdle were all of iron, and could be hooked to the *slabhraidh*, or iron chain that always dangled down the chimney over the fire to be brought into requisition for the oven, the pot, the kettle or the girdle as might be required. For oven-scones and cakes you had to pile fragments of glowing peat on to the iron lid of the oven so that the heat was even, all round.

And you regulated the heat by hooking your oven higher or lower on the *slabhraidh* as the case might require. One way and another we fared well.

George Macleod's little shop, as I say, did not provide our daily bread, but it had its distinct uses and we were grateful for it. It would seldom fail you for sugar and salt; for leather to repair your boots and shoes, and laces to keep them on; for candles and paraffin to light you through the winter; for soap and washing soda; for bogie-roll tobacco and matches; sometimes for tea and sugar and large hard biscuits.

Well, what more did you need when George Ross's spring-cart came weekly from Ullapool with quite a range of groceries? I liked to be around when he was due, for he almost always gave me two huge round toffees for which the modern name would probably be "gob-stoppers". I called them "Ross's potatoes", because when he introduced me to them he had remarked, "You'll not grow potatoes like these in Elphin." Mind you, he did not say that they actually were potatoes, for he was a good Free Presbyterian and would not mislead his customers — even though there was no "Sales Protection Act" to safeguard them from such deceptions. But I never knew their right name, so I called them by his.

I think nostalgically of them over the years and regard them as the finest productions of the confectioner's art — not so much perhaps for their sweetness as for their lastingness. The proper length of a sermon by the reckoning of an old Seceder lady was "twa big pandrops, slow-sooked and no' chawed." Consumed according to that method, "Ross's potatoes" would set a stiff test even for an old-world Seceder!

It seemed to me that the the tempo of life in Elphin in those days was, in all the circumstances, just right. We were almost all self-employed, so there was no one to judge whether we were late or early. As a self-contained community we decided our own time-tables. The nearest policeman in our parish was stationed at Lochinver, more than 20 miles away; and it seemed to me that his only duty among us was to be present on sheep-dipping days to ensure that the law, in this respect, was complied with.

Once Spring came there was, of course, plenty to do; ploughing, harrowing, sowing, planting — all with due regard to the correct rotation of crops. The lambing season presented its own claims, which were dutifully met. There was always anxiety about *sneachd nan uan* — the lamb's snow; for Spring always seemed to let Winter have its final fling at that time. The weather could be boisterous, and the lambing toll heavy.

Then there was the peat-cutting time, for we produced our own fuel as well. This operation had to be timed with seasonal accuracy, for if it was carried through too early in the year there was a risk that frost would spoil the soft peat; whereas too late a beginning might overlap with our early harvesting and jeopardise the ingathering of the hay-crop.

I loved the casting part in the peat-work far more than the cutting. It was relatively easy to *cut* the peat — especially where the moss was black and soft; but *casting* was quite another matter. You had to use your spreading-space to good advantage, and this called for a high degree of accuracy. There was an art in it. You cast your peat with a swing that only practice could produce, to bring it down in the precise place at which you had aimed. And when the cast extended to eight or nine peats in a row where every peat had to lie close to its neighbour, the feat required both skill and strength. But a well-spread peat-bank was a pleasing sight which went far to compensate the toil of producing it.

And the *al fresco* meals on *latha buain na moine* (peat-cutting day) — who could ever forget them? The glowing fire kindled with dry heather and sustained by *caorans* of last year's cutting; the hard-boiled eggs, the oatcakes and girdle scones, replete with lashings of fresh butter from our own churns, with appetites to match. The groaning tables of Dives himself never offered better fare.

Is maith an cocair an t-acras, 'S mairg a ni tarcuis air biadh, Ach fuarag eorn' an sail mo bhroig' Be'm biadh a b'fhearr a fhuair mi riamh.

(A good cook is the hunger and few would disparage good food. But a cold barley mash in the heel of my boot was the best food that ever I took).

So, reputedly, wrote the starving Highlander, a fugitive in the Peninsular War, after he had partaken of cold-water barley porridge that he had made for himself in the heel of his boot for lack of a more conventional utensil. Our appetite on the peat-moss was not as sharp as his, for our need was less pressing. But we fully understood what he meant. Hunger is indeed a good cook, and what better to produce it than a good day at the peats?

When the pressures of seasonal occupation eased off in the summer-lull the services of the crofters were often in requisition by the neighbouring hotels and shooting lodges as ghillies. The local lochs were excellent for brown trout, but the water-falls between them and the sea were too high for the salmon to leap. Loch Veyatie required two ghillies for the more distant beat; outboard motors were almost unknown in those days. It happened occasionally then that I was asked to act as the second ghillie.

Those were great occasions. Rowing was a marvellous exercise, and angling a great skill, and here the two combined. The older ghillies were real professionals and they entered heartily into the work. Apart from other considerations, the trays at the hotel which, at the close of the day, displayed the best catches reflected credit upon angler and ghillie alike. As good sportsmen, those ghillies loved to serve an expert; but, woe betide the bungler! The *sotto voce* criticisms of the ghillies - in Gaelic, of course — were tersely-worded and decidedly unflattering to say the least! On occasions, intense irritation expressed itself in biting sarcasm. On one of these occasions, when a good ghillie had been assigned to a very poor angler, whose ineptitude was matched only by his self- confidence, matters came to a head. On the long pull to the head of the loch he was using a minnow, and kept getting caught in shingle and underwater vegetation. More than once, his ghillie suggested firmly but politely that the weights on his tackle were too heavy, but he would have none of it. He was out for the heavier fish, and he knew what he was doing!

The ghillie resumed his rowing, but mischievously edged the boat into shallower water. The fisherman's reel suddenly screamed into action and the rod bent almost double.

"Steady, steady," cried the angler to the man on the oars, "I've hooked a big one."

The ghillie reversed his stroke, and the boat slowed down.

"Aye, aye," he said in accents of heavy scorn, "you've got a big one this time. *You've hooked aal Scotland.*"

But the minnow, when skilfully extricated, revealed that it had suffered serious damage in its endeavour to take "aal Scotland" in tow, and it was replaced by a smaller and lighter one — with more satisfactory results.

The same ghillie on another occasion served a Jew, an army man who could use a rod with skill, but who had unpleasant propensities that certainly did not enhance his reputation with the ghillies. They assumed that his wife – a charming lady – was of the same nationality, so, as they plied their oars, they conversed softly in Gaelic, and were by no means sparing of their Jewish employer, while he and his wife conversed on things in general.

All went well until the rods and baskets were safely stored in the car and the scion of Jacob had taken his place behind the wheel and started the engine. His wife slipped across for a final word with the ghillies.

"*Slan leibh,*" she whispered, "*chord an la rium gu math. 'S ann agaibh tha a'Ghaidhlig ghrinn. Moran taing.*" ("Good-bye, I greatly enjoyed the day. It's yourselves that have the excellent Gaelic. Many thanks.")

And with a roguish smile and wave she was gone.

What the ghillies said when they came to is not recorded!

It turned out that she was a Scotswoman with an Argyllshire background. Notwithstanding her early change of residence to London she had not lost the language of her forebears.

Our range of travel in those days was distinctly limited. Annual holidays were regarded as refinements of urban life which were quite surplus to the requirements of people who enjoyed the very best amenities of rusticity. In any case the conditions of travel were daunting. Road construction and maintenance in Sutherland had been slow and inadequate.

Away back in the end of the 18th century, William MacKenzie, the parish minister of Assynt, in his contribution to *The Statistical Account of Scotland*, deals at some length with travel difficulties in the county of Sutherland, and particularly in his own parish.

The area "from Assynt to Dornoch," he tells us, "is in tolerable degree opened up." And he puts in a strong plea for the construction of a road from Lairg to Alt-nan-Cealgach, a provision, as he urges, that would open up the wide expanse of moorland between these points, and bring the road from the East and the South to the very border of Assynt.

This road must have become a reality sooner, perhaps, than he had expected, for his successor, Rev. Charles Gordon, who was inducted in 1825, writes enthusiastically about "our excellent roads" and the advantages that they brought to the people. But their quality had not kept pace with the demands of improving transport, and in 1909, when first I passed over them, they could hardly be described as "excellent". By then the mail-car had taken over from the horse-drawn vehicle and "breakdowns" were not uncommon. The wiseacres shook their heads and said, "The sooner they bring back the horses the better".

But the sturdy Albion wagonettes that carried the mails were not to be blamed; the fault lay with the roads. The solid tyres of the heavy vehicles often cut such deep ruts in the road that further progress was impossible. The stretch between Oykel and Alt-nan-Cealgach was particularly bad. For those miles the road ran across a peaty bogland that reminded one of John Bunyan's description of the Slough of Despond which, says Bunyan, simply swallowed up "the twenty-thousand cart-loads of materials that had been cast into it, but remained the Slough of Despond still."

But, unlike Bunyan's *Slough* the *Mointeach* (peatland) has been conquered at last, and a good modern road has taken the place of the loose-gravelled hazard of earlier days.

"Is there much more of this wretched road?" enquired a pioneer motorist of a local man who was helping him out of a difficulty. "There is that, Sir," was the reply, "and it gets worse farther on. You'd better choose which rut you want, for you'll be in it almost all the way to Alt-nan-Cealgach."

I often cycled that part of the road, and the journey was quite a feat of skill — especially when the ruts were full of water or snow. The central part of the road, which alone served the cyclist's purpose, was seldom more than twenty inches wide. It required great dexterity to stay on, and it was a near disaster to slip off that centre!

But if it was "excellent" when Charles Gordon referred to it a century and a half ago, improvements had not kept pace with the years. Let us give the pioneers their due as today we bowl easily over the really good roads that they made possible, and do for them what we are enjoined to do for Wade and his men with whose Great North Road they were eventually linked:

> *If you'd seen these roads before they were made,*
> *You'd lift up your hands and bless General Wade.*

The fact that Ullapool was our nearest sea-port and shopping-centre meant that we visited it fairly frequently; so frequently indeed that, sitting here at my desk, I can still recall every bend and brae and bridge in its sixteen tortuous miles, from the ascent of Knockan Brae to the long descent from Morefield into Ullapool. And well I might. I have walked it, cycled it, motor-cycled it, motored it, covered it on horse-back and by cart, and it is from this wealth of experience that I pronounce the last-mentioned mode of transportation to be incomparably the best. But there are conditions to be observed. First, you must make your journey in summer or autumn when there is a fair chance of a really good day. Then you must have three or four bulging wool-sacks between you and the hard floor of the cart. And there, seated, reclining, or lying prostrate in the gully between the topmost wool-sacks, you might well be the envy of kings.

In the nature of things, of course, such heights of luxurious travel could be enjoyed only once in the round of the year, after the annual sheep-clipping, when the crofters were sending away their wool-yield for the year by the MacBrayne boat to the wool-merchants in Glasgow.

I well remember the day when my Uncle Sandy remarked laconically to me, "I was thinking of going to Ullapool with the wool one day next week. You are on holiday from school, so perhaps you would like to come with me."

"*Perhaps!*" I could hardly be more excited than if he had proposed a trip to New Zealand, which for some unaccountable reason, I then regarded as the most desirable part of the world to go to, but, of course, only for a visit. I had been hearing so much about the vagrant ecclesiastic from Assynt, Norman MacLeod, who finally settled there, as to conclude that the place which had won

Norman's ultimate approval, and for residence proved his final choice, must be high in the list of attractive homelands.

The day that had been chosen for our excursion turned out to be the ideal kind for our purpose. The old cart, with trusty *Star* between the shafts made slow progress, for it was heavy and springless, with iron-rimmed wheels that clacked noisily on their axle all the way. Since that eventful day I have travelled by comfortable observation cars and coaches, in this and other lands, but for observation facilities, I have never known anything to surpass that well-upholstered seat atop my uncle's croft-cart. And *Star*'s leisurely pace was just right for what, to me, was the paramount purpose of the day — to roll back my boundaries, and make a fuller acquaintance with my new environment.

The memory of it has never lost its thrill. There was Knockan Rock, with its marvellous panorama of lochs and streams, of mountains and moorland and Drumrunie, with its vast expanse of purple heather and rhododendron. Then came Strath Kanaird, with its trim houses and tidy crofts and Ardmair with its curving bay and pebbly beach. Lastly, the road climbed in long ascent to Morefield ridge with the enchanting outlook to the Summer Isles. The crofts on both sides of Loch Broom, ripening for an early harvest, looked like a huge stretch of patchwork quilting: and, nestling in the centre of this clash of countless shades of colour, lay the the trim little town of Ullapool, with the *Chieftain*, which was to ship our wool to Glasgow, tied up at the pier.

Ships always thrilled me, and do still. Once, a kindly Captain had made my schoolboy heart race with excitement by taking me aboard his craft, the *Adam Smith*; but it was only a coaling boat, calling in at Maningtree in Essex, where I was on a short holiday from London at the time. But on that first visit to Ullapool, I was actually taken aboard a real passenger ship, and even treated to a meal. It was the climax to a memorable day's outing, but it completely spoiled my sense of comparative dimensions. For, since that day, I have crossed the seas and oceans by some of the largest and fastest and best-equipped passenger liners then in service, but none of them came up to my boyish memory of MacBrayne's *Chieftain*, with its splendid figure-head of a kilted Highlander, dwarfing all the craft that surrounded it in the little harbour of Ullapool!

On our return journey, we lacked the comforts of our outward trip, for sacks of oatmeal and flour, and boxes of groceries, are not comparable with sacks of wool as travel comforts. But it had been a great day.

4: The Church of my Youth

As I look back I recall that I was not long in Sutherland when I came to realise that, somehow, the Church and the people were closer to each other in Scotland than seemed to be the case South of the Border. But it took me longer to understand that this was of the very essence of Scottish Presbyterianism. There was no ecclesiastical hierarchy, no graded clergy in the Scottish Reformed Church. The only priesthood recognised in the Church was "the priesthood of all believers", and, all down the years, the Scottish people had gone through fire and water in their resistance to the impositions of Rome and Canterbury alike. The stain of martyr-blood was upon moorland and mountain, and the people's Covenants had bound them together in defence of the Faith whereby God had revived the soul of the nation.

The subsequent wrangling within the National Church after the Revolution Settlement of 1690, and the restoration of Patronage in 1712, had disintegrating effects, and by the time of the Disruption in 1843 it was widely realised that the time had come for the re-building of the walls of Zion. Some of the dissenting bodies came together in 1847 to form the United Presbyterian Church, and talks for further re-union were soon under way. By and large, their reasons for breaking with the State had been similar. Had the time come for them to get together again? How did they now compare in respect of doctrine?

They decided to inquire, and it early became evident that the area of agreement was not as extensive as had been supposed, and in 1871 the conferring parties were instructed to confine their attention to the question of closer co-operation between the churches, rather than union.

In 1879 the United Presbyterian Church passed a Declaratory Act the purpose of which was to relax subscription of the Westminster Confession of Faith. In 1892, the Free Church General Assembly, by a large majority, stepped into line with the United Presbyterians by passing a similar measure, thereby facilitating the projected Church Union which eventually took place in 1900.

But meanwhile in the North of Scotland, Separatism, which was a vigorous reaction from Moderatism, had developed a censoriousness that embittered the Christian relations of better days. In the larger and more widely scattered congregations lay-preachers, catechists and teachers helped with the maintenance of Gospel ordinances among the people, but sometimes with a regrettably divisive influence.

This was particularly the case in the parish of Assynt. John Kennedy had gone there as assistant to William MacKenzie, to whom reference has previously been made in these pages. Kennedy was already showing promise of the fruitfulness which was to bring him renown as minister of Killearnan. Several professed conversion under his preaching, and Assynt seemed set for a time of blessing. The promise was not belied. As well as winning many for Christ, John Kennedy restored the respect of the people for the holy office in which he served. The cry of the penitent and the song of the pardoned became familiar sounds. *"The time of singing of birds was come, and the voice of the turtle was heard in the land."* The result was that by the time the Evangelicals formed the Free Church of Scotland in 1843, Moderatism was practically a spent force in the community although, unhappily, Separatism lingered on.

The first Free Church minister in Assynt was Rev. Charles Gordon, a man whose ministry was greatly blessed. Under Separatism some of the people had developed a decided anti-clerical spirit, and would be hard to please, no matter who might be chosen for the pastorate. But Neil Macleod (*Niall Ban*) settled the matter. "Arise", he counselled, "and anoint him, for this is he." So they chose Charles Gordon, to their own spiritual enrichment and the lasting benefit of Assynt.

It gave me great satisfaction in school-days to find that the old people of Assynt could still recall Neil Macleod, and that he was honourably mentioned both in *Disruption Worthies of the Highlands* and *Annals of the Disruption*. Rev. Eric Findlater, of Lochearnhead, in his sketch of Neil in the *Annals*, describes him as his *"beau-ideal* of the apostle John - the loving disciple." Neil Macleod was my great, great grandfather and, vaguely, I cherished the hope that, somehow, the relationship — distant though it was — might secure some spiritual benefit for me!

My grandmother's stories about him used to attract me greatly. She and her chums would gather to his house, of an afternoon, and play their games around him, to his quite evident pleasure, and then he would gather them to him as far as his arms would reach and tell them Bible stories and pray with them. She lived to a good old age and crossed the century; and still, as she recalled the distant days of childhood, a wistful but happy look came into her face.

The warm after-glow of Charles Gordon's ministry was still discernible in Assynt at the end of the century, and indeed it had been revived by the devoted service of William MacDonald, a native of Skye, whose coming to Elphin was the means of bringing blessing to many. William was somewhat deformed in his feet and his incapacity for the normal fishing and agricultural occupations of the Highlands necessitated his taking up an alternative calling. He became a tailor, and appears to have pursued his chosen trade in rather itinerant fashion. This meant that he was able to form the acquaintance of many notable Christians in the Highland area and to become known to the Church Committee who had a special responsibility for the Christian benefit of the Highlands.

The call to service in Elphin came to him in a quite remarkable manner.

He was serving at Kirkhill, Inverness-shire at the time, and a Bible-class which he had built up was showing great promise when the direction came to him to proceed to Assynt. The idea of leaving his Bible-class just when it seemed they needed him most, and to go to a people of whom he knew next to nothing seemed utterly wrong, and he resisted it strongly.

The answer seemed to come to him in a dream, and it was to the effect that he *should go to Elphin*. As for the young people in his Bible-class about whom he was so concerned, God would look after them. The voice that spoke to him seemed to say quite audibly, "Not one of them shall ever utter a cry in hell."

It was Dr. John Macleod who first told me about William MacDonald's Bible-class. We were sitting in his vestry in the Free North Church, Inverness, and the story was interrupted by the arrival of the church officer to escort us to the pulpit for the second service.

"I will tell you the rest after the service," said Dr. Macleod. "But meanwhile," he added, "have a glance at a pew to your left (and he indicated precisely where it was) and you will see two elderly ladies sitting there if they are well enough to be in church today."

"Well, did you see them?" he asked when we returned to the vestry. I replied that I had, and he resumed the interrupted story.

"Those ladies," he said, "are the last surviving members of William MacDonald's Bible-class. I knew a number of them, and they all bore evidence of saving-grace."

It would seem that William MacDonald's dream had been

translated into reality, and his service to Christ became even more fruitful after his removal to Elphin where he remained for the rest of his days. A tombstone of red granite marks his last resting-place in the little road-side grave-yard above Loch Cama.

As a schoolboy I used to dabble in simple photography and, learning that one much-envied lady in the district possessed a photograph of him, I asked permission to copy it. Surprisingly, the result of my effort was so good that several of the older people begged me to make copies for them also. And so it came about that memories of a saintly man were revived among a people whom he had served so devotedly for many years.

During my Edinburgh ministry I had another remote contact with William MacDonald's work. I was calling one day to see an elder who, by then, was almost blind. Archie Macleod (for that was his name) was from Waternish in Skye, but had spent most of his life in the South. Picking up a book that lay to his hand – *Sermons by the Rev. Malcolm Forbes of Portmahomack* — he asked, "Do you have a copy of this book?"

I replied that I had not.

"Then," he said, "I'll be glad if you'll accept it. It is a great favourite of mine, but I can no longer read it, and I would like it to go to someone who would value it."

I accepted it gratefully and, turning to the flyleaf, was astonished to read the words inscribed on it:-

"William MacDonald, Elphin.
Given to me by Ann MacLeod, Elphin."

"How did you come by this book?" I asked.

"It was given to me by a daughter of that William MacDonald, " he replied. "He was my uncle."

"Well," I said, "it happens that the Ann MacLeod who gave him the book is my aunt."

Archie was delighted that the book, given to his uncle by my aunt Ann, was now in my hands.

Some time later I asked my aunt if she could remember having given Mr. MacDonald this gift.

"Yes," she said, "I bought two copies of it with my very first wages after I left home; one for my father, and the other for Mr. MacDonald."

She too was thrilled to know that it was now in my possession.

"You must have been strongly attached to him to give him such a gift from your very first wages," I remarked.

"I was," she replied, with a betraying emotion, "and I will always remember him."

So the William MacDonald who had been so reluctant to leave Kirkhill had not lost his charm for young people when, at what he had come to regard as a call to duty, he had left his beloved Kirkhill for the colder uplands of Assynt.

Regrettably, a divisive spirit entered the church life of the parish towards the end of his service there. The move for Church Union was afoot and the people were taking sides. A forced union was bearing the bitter fruit of discord and division. The minister during the time of the Declaratory Act movement in 1892 was Rev. Norman Mackay, and his tepid leadership had been largely responsible for a secession into the Free Presbyterian movement. Altogether, the situation brought about in Elphin by this period of change was that the Free Church of 1843 was divided into three parts; the Free Presbyterian Church of 1893, the United Free Church of 1900, and the continuing Free Church of Scotland. A dispersion instead of a union!

The Free Church minority persisted with its dissent from the Declaratory Act, claiming that the large majority who had tried to bulldoze them out of the Free Church had succeeded only in un-churching themselves. And the House of Lords, when appealed to, upheld the claim. The name "Free Church of Scotland", it was declared, "belonged to the minority who, holding to the Church's Constitution and Standards, had declined to be a party to a compromising Union."

A period of controversy ensued, and this was the ecclesiastical situation in Sutherland when I arrived there in 1909.

The wranglings over Church Union had had at least the good effect of creating a new interest in the Church and its message. That man was indeed a "stranger in Jerusalem" who knew not "the things that had come to pass there in those days." The people took sides over the matters at issue, and felt it incumbent upon them to do so intelligently. The *Shorter Catechism* they already knew, at least by memory. They were familiar with its masterly definitions of Christian doctrine even if they could not fully grasp their meaning. And if the *Confession of Faith* was widely regarded as rather "beyond" them, the pulpit message to which they were accustomed was impregnated with its teaching. The district catechising was long past before I went to Assynt, but its effect was still to be found in the older people who had grown up under it. In their fireside conversations they kept themselves abreast of the trend of events in the ecclesiastical arena, and few of them were better informed than our esteemed elder, Duncan MacRae.

Duncan, who was converted in early life, had sat at the feet of some of the most notable preachers of the time. He had a fine discernment, a retentive memory, and a marked theological cast of mind, which he developed by his reading. He was early accepted into the fellowship of some of the most eminent office bearers in the neighbouring parishes and was the means of bringing many of them to our own communion gatherings in Elphin.

Duncan was a winsome Christian. I remember well my first meeting with him, for he was one of the very first to greet me when I arrived in Elphin. He was a man of spare build and medium height. Already ageing, his tufty dark hair and beard were streaked with grey. His right arm shook from a palsy that had laid him low some time before, but he had made a good, though not complete, recovery. When speaking English, which he could do very correctly, he chose his words with care. "The Gaelic" was his native tongue. The slight stammer that sometimes affected him — although never when he was leading in prayer or conducting a meeting – seemed to add a pleasing quality to his speech. And there was a soft music to his voice such as you might have heard in the voices of the bards of long ago.

In the Church troubles of 1900 and after, Duncan had been an ardent Constitutionalist and, in the crippling depletion of ministerial strength that the Free Church had suffered, the elders of the Church were often called upon to fill the vacant pulpits. Duncan was one of them; but he would never presume to – literally – "occupy the pulpit", nor deliver a sermon of his own composing. He took a modest view of his own attainments and always dreaded lest he should unwittingly stray from the path of sound doctrine. So, when it came to sermon-time, we could never be sure who was to be the preacher of the day!

Very often it was Thomas Boston of Ettrick, for many of his discourses had been translated into Gaelic and were prime favourites – especially his *Fourfold State* — with the good people of Sutherland. Or it might be, and often was, Robert Murray M'Cheyne of Dundee, for some of his sermons also had been translated. Occasionally, we were treated to a discourse from John Owen, the great Puritan; or one of the Erskine brothers, Ebenezer or Ralph.

Duncan MacRae had a pleasant reading voice, and although he was innocent of the art of elocution he could hold the attention of his audience. True, there were times when the sound of a car grinding its way noisily up Knockan Brae had the effect of turning the eyes of the younger set to the plain-glass windows of the Church, for a car was still a rather rare sight in those parts, especially on the Sabbath Day. But there are some of the youthful hearers of those times who, as they read their M'Cheyne in later years, hear again those tender appeals in the tremulous voice of Duncan MacRae, and feel their power all the more on that account.

Duncan was a stickler for punctuality, even to his old age. Almost at the same minute every Sabbath morning we could see his plaid-clad figure on his way to the Church, usually the first there. Sometimes he went with grave misgivings. Who was he to take upon himself this sanctuary service? Once, at least, this question was answered for him in a most remarkable way. He told us about it over a meal later in the day.

On his way to Church that morning he was overtaken by a local halfling — a poor man with scarcely the intellect of a little child. He was completely incapable of receiving instruction, even to the extent of being able to dress himself, although his garb was of the simplest kind – a long skirt-like kilt with a loose jacket to match. But he always went to Church and was among the first to arrive. I firmly believe now that God communicated more to his poor simple mind than we ever imagined. But that by the way.

Duncan was rather downcast in spirit that morning, the church reponsibility had been weighing heavily upon him and he had been praying about it, but without an answer. When therefore the simpleton overtook him, Duncan said — just for the sake of talking to somebody – "I wish you had a good word for a poor man, Murdo." "I have that", was the unexpected reply. "What is it then?" asked Duncan. "*Urnaigh nam bochd bheir e fainear, 'S cha diult E iad le tair.*" ("The prayer of the destitute, He surely will regard."), came the answer. "I took it as from the Lord", concluded Duncan, "for I knew that it could not possibly be of man."

That a prophet is not without honour save amongst his own people is an oft-verified affirmation, but it did not apply to our worthy elder. The people admired him, not only because of his personal qualities, but because of the courageous stand he had made in the time of the Church's recent crisis. He was not really bitter about those who had left the Free Church to set up another denomination in the district, but sometimes his words could be edged with irony. "A queer Union", he once said, "they left the Church of their fathers to unite with the United Presbyterians, and there is not a single United Presbyterian to unite with!"

Meeting a young minister of the new party one day, he enquired as to why he kept such a huge dog, for the enormous hound had been bounding around them as they talked.

"To gather again the flock that you scattered." was the answer. *"Tional a'choin duibh!"* (the gathering of the black dog) came the immediate retort, "That is the kind of gathering that goes on today with your *Union* movements. But when the dispersed of Israel are eventually gathered into one, it won't be by the driving of the black dog, but by the drawing of the Holy Spirit."

By far the most important week in the round of the year in Elphin was the Communion week. It fell in mid-summmer when the countryside looked at its very best. The weather, as I remember it, was usually fine. The lochs, so often ruffled by the winds that swept down on them from the mountain gullies, placidly reflected the tree-fringed islands and the bracken-clad slopes of the girdling hills. The higher ranges, so often the battle-fields of warring elements, kept silent sentinel over the assembling people, reminding us that "as the mountains are round about Jerusalem, so the Lord is round about His people from henceforth and for ever."

No public-service vehicle ran through Elphin, but one from Ullapool to Coigach brought passengers to within five miles of the hamlet, leaving them to complete the journey on foot, or perhaps by cart. The Lairg to Lochinver mail-car brought our passengers from those areas to the Ledmore cross-roads – only around two miles away. Often, on the Wednesday before the Communion services began, some of us – if the weather was good — used to climb a hill where we had a panoramic view of the approach roads from Knockan Rock on the one side and Ledmore on the other, to see if we could spot any dark-garbed people converging on the township.

Where the visitors were accommodated during the days of the Communion season we could never understand. The houses were small, and the families large; but, as yet, there were no crops gathered into the barns, and shake-downs were available to the younger set, greatly to their delight. And anyway, "love makes room" as the old folks used to say.

The ministers who shared the Communion services stayed with Duncan and usually the "Interim Moderators", who looked after the affairs of the congregation during the long vacancy in the pastorate, deferred largely to his judgement. He had his own special favourites, but he was always ready to admit a newcomer to his inner circle. The Free Church had many vacancies in those early post-union years, and in her eagerness to meet the needs of pastorless congregations as soon as possible, she had perhaps been too trusting in some of the admissions to her ministry. A few of these newcomers proved themselves to be mere birds of passage who, before long, found better feathered nests in the Established Church, with the result that the younger ministers of the Church were apt to be regarded with some caution until they proved their worth. But Duncan's judgements were charitable, notwithstanding the disappointments he had experienced from the men referred to.

One in particular of these defectors had grieved him. He had succeeded to the pulpit of one of the best known 1900 Constitutionalists — Rev. John Noble, of Lairg — and Duncan had expected great things of him. But he had gone, and Duncan's confidence in the younger ministry had been shaken; and ours too! So much so that when shortly afterwards we had a young minister at our Communion whose smile was so ready that, at times, it came out in the pulpit, we wondered what to make of it. Was this another of the "light brigade"?

By the end of the Fellowship meeting on Friday Duncan's mind was made up. The young stranger had "closed the question" in a way that had revealed an extensive experimental acquaintance with the changeful experiences of the Christian life, and with the "marks" of true grace. Our elder's face was eloquent of deep approbation. *"Chan fhalbh am fear sin"*, ("That one won't go away") he declared with conviction.

And he was right. The said minister, Rev. J. Mackay Maclennan, M.A., had fruitful pastorates in two charges, covering more than fifty years, before resigning his ministry, and had been elected Moderator of the General Assembly which met in Glasgow in 1938 to mark the tercentenary of the famous Covenanting Assembly which met there in 1638, under the Moderatorship of Alexander Henderson of Leuchars, when they abolished Episcopacy and restored Presbyterian polity in accordance with the demands of the Scottish people.

If the truth be told, we of the younger set in Elphin made very little of the Friday "Question Meeting" in Communion week, but we would not have missed it for anything; it was so unusual. It began in the familiar Church-service style; but when the opening exercises of worship were over the senior minister would invite one of the brethren to "give out a passage of Scripture that would be suitable for the purposes of the day" — which were self-examination and testimony.

Who would respond? We waited not less anxiously than the minister himself, although — it may be presumed — for different reasons; for the presiding minister was expected to give an impromptu introduction to the passage proposed, and perhaps suggest lines of thought that might lead to profitable speaking.

Much of what was said was, of course, lost on us, but we came away with very definite ideas as to who were the "stars" of the occasion, the principal criteria being (a) the fluency of the speaker, and (b) the length of time for which he spoke.

Alas for the shallow judgements of callow youth!

The visiting elders who gathered to us during the communion season came from the surrounding parishes. What a variety of types they represented! One of them, Angus Munro from the Dornoch area, had an unusual attraction for me, perhaps because he spoke Gaelic in the East Coast idiom and I had not heard it before. But, for some reason, he always sent my thoughts to the Apostle John.

Once, to the consternation of Duncan, he was late in arriving. What had happened to delay him? The story eventually leaked out.

He had come some ten miles of his journey on his usual day when the Tempter began to whisper to him. "What a hypocrite you are! On Friday you will be speaking of brotherly love and forbearance as characteristics of the true Christian. And yet, only yesterday, you quarrelled with your neighbour about a peat-bank!"

The tempted man defended himself on the ground that it was the *neighbour* who had picked the quarrel, and that he himself had only stood up for his own *rights*.

"*Rights*", taunted the Tempter, "and you profess to be a disciple of Him Who said, 'Whosoever shall smite thee on thy right cheek, turn to him the other also.'"

The Adversary, it would seem, meant to keep him back from the Communion or lay him under bondage for the duration of his visit. But Angus was not having it! Turning back, he sought out the estranged neighbour, conceded to him the rights that he had so arrogantly claimed, and begged his pardon for having spoken back so sharply to him the previous day.

That matter settled, he set out again for the Communion on the following day, thus arriving a day late. But all the discerning people present were agreed that the good man's branch was especially heavy with dew when he took part in the Friday meeting. And, at the time, Duncan MacRae alone knew the story behind it!

The early morning prayer-meetings of the Communion season drew some of the younger people also: again, probably just because of the novelty of them: for to set out for church before eight o'clock on a week-day morning was, to say the least, something out of the usual. I think I must have attended them all, but then I lived near the church.

The morning air was sweet with the mingled scents of the wild flowers that brushed our feet as we walked through the crofts. All was quiet except for the harmonious chorus of the birds singing their morning praise. The good men who shared the devotions of those early meetings were so obviously under the impression of Divine things that, somehow, it seemed good to be among them.

The climax, of course, was the dispensation of the Sacrament on the Lord's Day. On rare occasions, the service was held out of doors, although I cannot remember having attended more than once. Our place of meeting was not so well suited to the purpose as were, for instance, *Leabaidh na Ba Bainne* (Bed of the White Cow), in Gairloch, the sheltered Ferintosh Burn and the Migdale Communion hollow in Creich. It was not so well enclosed as these, with the result that undisciplined eyes and ears were particularly liable to distraction. It was a scene, however, that one would like to transfer to canvas − *the cailleachs* in their sober blacks and close-fitting bonnets or frilled *currachds*; the *bodachs* also in their sartorial best, some with tasselled smoking caps, or plain white handkerchiefs on their heads to give protection from the heat of the sun or the disturbing attention of stinging insects; and away at the front the 'box' or portable pulpit which housed the preachers. In the background the Knockan River seemed to blend its slow *cronan* with the grave sweet melody of the Gaelic Psalms, led by full-voiced precentors who, on this occasion, were Murdo Kerr from Lochinver, and William Munro from Drumbeg.

The climax was reached when, after the "fencing" of the Lord's Table, the communicants began to move forward to take their places. What did it mean? Some of us knew, and wished we didn't; it left us uncomfortable. Deep down in our hearts, we knew that those who were gathering to the empty seats that had been set at the front were professing their faith in Christ, and those who remained behind signified by so doing that they were none of His. And we were among them!

Over the years I can still see Duncan MacRae, assisted by elders from other congregations serving the Table. A stickler for correctness, he quietly saw to it that all things were done decently and in order. And when (but alas! it too seldom happened) a new communicant was seen at the Table, it was evident from his very

countenance that his enjoyment of the Communion was thereby
enriched. And when the congregation sang the closing verses of
Psalm 72, with which the Communion service invariably ended, his
heart was with *"the son of Jesse"* in his great doxology:

> *The whole earth let His glory fill*
> *Amen, so let it be.*

The Monday service of the Communion season was a wistful
occasion for those good people, for it meant the parting of the ways
for another year. But there was a lingering gladness too, and a joyful
anticipation of eternal and perfect communion in which all the
saints shall yet be joined.

"I'm saying with Jane Armadale today," I once heard Duncan
remark after a Monday service, "Thank the Lord, there will be no
Monday to the communion in heaven."

5: The Church and its Youth

Rural isolation has its compensations, but its disadvantages also, and it is sometimes difficult to assess the ultimate balance. Some of the drawbacks bear particularly upon the religious training of the young people. They call for and deserve all the consecrated attention that can be bestowed upon them.

In my youth, Sabbath Schools and Bible Classes were almost unknown over wide areas of the Highlands and Islands, and there were many who did not regard this as a matter for regret. "The place for teaching the child is at the mother's knee," they would tell you: and to that declaration – which no right-thinking person would want to dispute – they had nothing to add. Questions arise, however, that ought to be deeply pondered. For instance, what happens when the child out-grows the height of the "parent's knee" standards? And when the parent is incapable of giving systematic instruction? Or when the parent has little or no concern for the spiritual development of the child? Even if religious instruction is dutifully and competently given in the home would it still not be beneficial for those young people to come together in the wider fellowship of the Sabbath School and Bible Class? I could answer some of those questions from personal experience.

In Elphin, Duncan MacRae conducted a Sabbath School single-handed. A pedagogue he certainly was not. His plan of instruction could scarcely be described as systematic – except, indeed, that in some things at least, he followed the memory work and readings prescribed in *The Instructor*. It was all sound teaching, the good man's heart was in it, and it was reinforced by his own life and example. Inevitably, in a class which represented different age groups one's gravity was sometimes strained. If we laughed he would reprove us solemnly, reminding us that we were studying God's Word in God's House. But I remember at least one occasion when his old face creased with a smile that defied repression, and when his reproof was broken with what sounded suspiciously like a chuckle.

We had been recapitulating briefly the lesson of the previous Sabbath. "We spoke of two Arks last week", he said, "Noah's Ark, and the Ark of the Covenant. What did Noah's Ark contain?"

Now, the previous Sabbath there had also been a passing allusion to Moses and his ark of bulrushes, and the dreamy laddie to whom the question was put was obviously confused.

"Please sir," he stammered, "Moses and beasts." But memory loves to linger over the lessons he returned to again and again — whatever the Welfare of Youth Committee might prescribe — the ineffable mystery of God manifest in the flesh; the unfathomable sorrow and horror that intermingled in the Gethsemane prayer; and, above all, the dazzling glory of the love that lay behind the atoning sacrifice of Calvary.

No, we cannot claim that our Sabbath school, judged by the recognised standards, was efficiently conducted. But we do claim that never did a teacher love his young charges more than Duncan MacRae did, nor take greater pains, within his limitations, to instruct them in the things that matter most.

As well as being our Sabbath School teacher, Duncan had a link with the day school. He was the attendance officer, more familiarly known as the *whipper-in*. The office was a complete sinecure as far as Elphin school was concerned: but the person holding it was expected to visit the school periodically and perform some minor duties. Duncan, however, was usually asked to render a service that lay outwith his office, namely, to lead us in prayer.

Now, a man who could do that was classed by us as far above ordinary mortals. It was therefore with some dismay that, after one of these visits we saw our football, misdirected by a careless kick, heading straight in his dircction as he walked down the road from the school. A warning shout was too late. The ball bounced off his plaid, leaving a muddy mark. For a moment we were silent. How would he take it? We need not have worried. Slowly pacing the short distance to where the misguided ball lay, he administered a vigorous kick that sent it unerringly in the direction of the offender and caught him squarely amidships. Nervous laughter greeted this unexpected display of marksmanship — laughter that grew in volume when we saw that Duncan was laughing too. That afternoon he was conveyed on his homeward walk by a small escort of admiring schoolboys.

Duncan never married, but his way with young folk revealed both sympathy and understanding. I recall an occasion when I was keen to go to a meeting of which I feared he might not approve.

"Why don't you ask me to go with you?" he asked when the matter was referred to him.

I was astounded by the very idea.

"Because I know you would not come," I replied.

"And do you think Christ would if He were here?"

"Oh no," I exclaimed shocked by the bare suggestion.

"Well then *mo bhalachan*, take this as your rule; don't ever go where you could not ask Him to go with you."

Those simple words often gave valued counsel long after my old friend was gathered to his fathers and I had left youth far behind.

It was my good fortune, although I did not regard it as so at the time, that after his paralysis had made it almost impossible for Duncan to use his pen he chose me as his amanuensis. He was often around our house and the arrangement was convenient. There, but more frequently in his own trim cottage, I used to write to his dictation the letters by which he kept in touch with his closest friends. I was often accorded the privilege of reading their letters to him. Those good men might have learned the art of letter-writing from Samuel Rutherford himself, for, while they lacked the finish of the famous Covenanter's luxuriant style, they had the similar characteristic of being rich in angel's food and fragrant with heavenly spices.

But they puzzled me. They seemed to be written in a code not decipherable to ordinary mortals. I thought of John Bunyan, listening to the poor women in Bedford as they spoke of the Christian life. "I heard," said Bunyan, "but I understood not, for they were far above, out of my reach; for their talk was about a new birth."

In like manner I read, but *"such knowledge was too wonderful for me; it was high, I could not attain unto it."*

But even yet, as I recall these letters, I think of the possibilities of a work for Christ through the ministry of the pen even in ordinary correspondence. What might we not accomplish for the kingdom of God if, instead of the inanities in which, too often, we indulge in our social correspondence we made these communications with our friends part of our witness for Christ!

"Then they that feared the Lord spake often one to another; and the Lord hearkened, and heard it, and a book of remembrance was written before Him for them that feared the Lord, and that thought upon His name." (Mal.3:16)

There was another Duncan in the eldership of the Assynt congregations, Duncan Kerr of Stoer. This Duncan was widely recognised, not only as a man of marked piety, but also of quite exceptional ability as a theologian. A bachelor, for a long time living alone, he had ample time and opportunity to sit at his precious books and assimilate their contents. The results of his diligence in this respect were clearly evident in his contributions to the Fellowship meetings at the Communion gatherings. There was a machine-gun rapidity in his utterance that sometimes left his hearers breathless as they tried to keep pace, but their pains were richly rewarded. I have seen Dr. Donald Munro bent low over the pulpit book-board in the Elphin church so as not to miss a word uttered by this remarkable man. In theological discussion he was unsurpassed among his contemporaries. Few had the temerity to throw down the gauntlet to him in theological disputation, but some did just to draw him out.

My fellow-student, John Mackenzie, later the much respected minister of Plockton and Kyle and then of Leverburgh, told me once of an encounter with him. Duncan sometimes had moods of depression and on one of these occasions John had called on him to see if he could chide him out of his dumps, but Duncan was resistant to all consolation.

When John visited him the following day, however, the clouds had lifted, and he asked Duncan what had given him such relief. The reply was, (and I translate it almost literally) "Well, the Lord spoiled this world on me, and I find it hard to believe He will spoil the next one on me also."

In other words, the Lord had so raised his affections to 'things above' that the 'things on earth' which used to engross him had lost their former fascination. He now sought, above all else, 'the kingdom of God and His righteousness' and faith revelled in the prospect of fulfilment.

"But", said John, just to try him out, "perhaps it wasn't like that. Perhaps it was just the trials that you have endured in providence that, as you say, spoiled this world on you."

Duncan's rejoinder was emphatic. "Not at all", he exclaimed, "what took my mind off this world was the glory that I saw in Christ Himself."

It is a testimony that every true believer will understand.

> *Turn your eyes upon Jesus,*
> *Look full in His wonderful face,*
> *And the things of earth will grow strangely dim*
> *In the light of His glory and grace.*

6: A Guided Walk

Climatic conditions in our quarter were never very dependable, even in the height of summer. Banks of low cloud, rolling in from the Minch, would quite suddenly drape the mountain tops, and sheets of rain, driving before the wind, would so flood the countryside that, within an hour or two, the trickling burns would become foaming torrents.

But the storm could just as suddenly pass; and, viewing the countryside, now smiling innocently under a cloudless sky, no one would ever believe that, so recently, Nature had been in such a fractious mood. The steep water-courses soon drained away the surplus water and, gladdened by the warm sunshine and the mingled perfumes arising from the refreshed meadows, one felt it was good to be alive.

It was on such an evening that Duncan MacRae made me his willing conscript for a walk along a half-track road that skirted the crofts. Rabbits thumped warningly to their young, and scampered headlong to their burrows, their white scuts bobbing as they ran. The birds joined in joyous chorus, the cuckoo, as it seemed, waiting for a break in their song before making her own mellifluous contribution. Young lambs competed in wild games for which there were no rules. The mountains and the hills were breaking out before us into singing, and all the trees of the field clapped their hands.

But my companion was thinking deep, deep thoughts of days that were now far away.

Stopping suddenly, and leaning on a wayside fence, he pointed me first to one house, and then to another — both now tenantless and one in complete ruin.

"Did I ever tell you about the conversion of *Merran Mhor*?" he asked. Actually he had, but I asked him to tell me again. The houses to which he had called my attention were *Merran*'s old home, and then the house where she had first encountered the Lord.

Merran, or Marion, Macleod had been a giddy, thoughtless young woman whose affections were squarely set on the world and what it offered. Church services and diets of catechising were definitely not in her line of interest, and her only reason for going to the meeting in the nearby house on that memorable evening was that she had newly acquired a showy dress from a relative in Glasgow, and even a dull religious meeting provided a good enough opportunity to show it off. So she waited until all the people were assembled and then made her ostentatious *debut*.

Donald MacKenzie, a local catechist, was in charge, and as she flounced by him the words of Jeremiah came unbidden to his mind, *"O, earth, earth, earth, hear the word of the Lord."* (Jer. 22:29)

Now, Donald had felt constrained to spend most of the preceding night in solitary prayer, and the following morning he confided to a friend his presentiment that"a breach would be made upon the kingdom of Satan that day."

The expectation was realised. Marion's new dress was rather crumpled before the service was over, for Donald MacKenzie's address had not proceeded far when she fell to the floor in a deep faint and had to be carried home. Deep conviction of sin followed. The proud young woman was humbled in sincere repentance. Comfort and consolation eventually came, as she told Donald MacKenzie, through a few words of Scripture which must have become lodged in her mind at one time or another, ". . . walk before God in the light of the living." (Ps. 56:13) *That*, she declared, by God's grace she was henceforth resolved to do.

Marion was almost illiterate: and now, for the first time in her life, she regretted it. Painstakingly, she applied herself to a study of words so as to advance herself in the knowledge of God's Word. Her nephew, Black Angus (*Aonghas Dubh*) was still alive when I went to Elphin, and he used to tell how annoyed he sometimes felt by his aunt's frequent requests that he should come and "read a chapter" to her. There were times when, in his haste to get it over, he would read quickly, and make mistakes. Marion would pull him up. *"Air do shocair a nis, cha'n ann mar sin tha e agam-sa"* (Easy now, that is not how I remember it), she would say. *"Read it again."* And she would quote correctly from memory what he was misquoting in his reading. Marion had to get it right; so much depended on accuracy when you were reading God's message.

Marion's "walk before the Lord in the light of the living" was free from all pretension, and so consistently maintained that many of the Lord's people took her as their model in the Christian life.

One of these was a young girl in Ullapool in whose home Marion used to stay while attending the Communion services there. The girl had recently become so conscious of indwelling corruption as to fear lest her profession of faith in Christ had been entirely false. No one whose mind could lodge such corrupt thoughts could possibly be a true Christian! She was sure that a genuinely good woman like Marion Macleod from Elphin was never so troubled in heart as she was. She would like to overhear her private devotions, but how could this be brought about?

A plan occurred to her. She had heard that Marion was rather a poor sleeper, and that she was accustomed to use her wakeful times in prayer. Now, her home was often so full at Communion times that beds had to be shared. Why not press for the privilege of sharing her bed with Marion?

The plan met with success, and the young woman awaited events. In the small hours of the morning her companion became restless and, after a while, slipped quietly out of bed and knelt beside it. The younger woman strained her ears, eager not to miss a whisper of Marion's supplications. But, to her profound amazement, all she heard was one entreaty, brokenly repeated again and again, "*A Thighearna, nach saor Thu mi bho'n ifrinn a tha'n taobh a stigh dhiom? Nach saor Thu mi bho'n ifrinn a tha'n taobh a stigh dhiom?*" (Lord, wilt Thou not save me from the hell that is within me?)

And then it began to dawn on the younger Christian that an increasing awareness of indwelling corruption was the inevitable accompaniment of growth in grace. And she was comforted.

Many years after hearing this story I used it as an illustration in a Gaelic sermon that I preached in the hall of the Free North Church, Inverness, during Dr. John Macleod's ministry, but without giving names. Mrs. Macleod was in the audience, and we walked back to the manse together.

"You took me back many years by your reference to Marion Macleod," she remarked.

"Had you heard it before?" I replied.

"More than that," she answered, "I was the young woman who shared Marion's bed with her."

Margaret Matheson of Ullapool, as she then was, was by no means the only young Christian to be helped by Marion.

In George MacDonald's *Men of Sutherland* there is a short supplement on *Godly Women of Sutherland*, in which Marion has an honoured place. This is how he sums her up: "Marion Macleod was a genuine Christian – solid, discerning and judicious – and had passed through deep waters of soul experience ere being firmly established in the faith of the Gospel. Several incidents in her Christian life are fraught with instruction to those seeking the way Zionward."

However, to return... Duncan and I moved on from Marion's old home and the place of her conversion, to finish our walk at his home. On the way he spoke about Neil (*Bain*) Macleod, for we passed nearby the ruins of his house. Neil's holy life, he said, had been a deterrent to evil in the community, and the good people of surrounding districts sought him out with their problems, for he was reckoned a veritable Greatheart by the younger pilgrims of his time.

But the evening was wearing late, and my old friend was tired and wistful. The youngest of a notable circle of Christians, he had lived to mourn their passing. "O to be wi' Ritchie!" cried Alexander Peden, when he thought of his fellow-Covenanter, Richard Cameron, so early called to his eternal reward. And a similar longing, I doubt not, often took possession of Duncan MacRae when he recalled in his closing years the companions of his pilgrimage in earlier times, as he had been doing that day.

There was one thing, and one thing only, that used to strain my relations with Duncan, and that was when he would suggest to me that God's purpose for my life was to serve in the ministry of the Gospel. It was not that I disparaged the ministry; far otherwise. Rather, it was that I deemed myself unworthy of such an exalted office. Besides, a man ought to be sure that he was called to the ministry; and how could he be sure? Had not the great "Mr Lachlan" (of Lochcarron) himself said, "*Cha deanar ministeir gun fhoghlum, ach och, och, cha dean foghlum ministeir.*" (A minister is not made without learning, but och, och, learning does not make a minister.)

When I told him that I was returning to London to study for another profession he told me bluntly that I was making a mistake, and even took the highly-esteemed Rev. Donald Munro, of Ferintosh, to see me in the hope that he would back him up.

"Do you think," asked Mr. Munro, coming immediately to the point when it was raised, "that you would be happier in journalism than you would in the ministry?"

Briefly, and unhesitatingly — for I had no wish to prolong the interview — I replied in the affirmative.

"Then," replied Mr. Munro, "don't let anyone persuade you to enter the ministry unless you feel called to it in a way that you cannot resist."

My heart blessed him for his wise counsel. That "call" eventually came, and when it did there was no resistance. Life could offer no greater honour, no richer reward, than to be "an ambassador of Christ."

Duncan had died before I reached that turning-point in life, but he seemed to know about it before I did!

He used to call at my Elphin home for news of me, and was kept informed of my progress, and of my enjoyment of my studies.

"That is good," he once remarked, "but if I am not mistaken, it is not there that he is to be trained for the work that the Lord has in view for him."

Of this conversation I knew nothing until after his death.

Our final parting had been in a little hollow on the hill-side, not far from his home.

"You will come no farther," he said. And there he committed me to God in prayer for daily guidance and blessing.

We shook hands in parting. "We shall never meet again on earth," he said. Protestingly, I indicated my intention to be back on holiday the following year, and expressed my hope to see him then.

He was silent for a moment, and then, "Perhaps you may see me," he said, "but I don't expect to see you."

I wondered what he meant but made no further comment.

As we went our different ways I looked back over the widening distance and watched as he passed over the ridge. With a backward glance and a wave of his hand he passed from my view.

When I returned the following year I was told that he had become very feeble and was confined to bed.

I resolved that I must see him in the morning. But before morning dawned he had been translated to where it is Eternal Day. In moments of mental cloudiness shortly before his passing, he imagined that he was serving at the Lord's Table. A friend asked him what he was singing, and he replied, *"Coleshill"*, and then feebly repeated the last lines of the first verse of Psalm 121:

> *O'n Dia rinn talamh agus neamh*
> *tha m' fhurtachd uile teachd.*
>
> *(My safety cometh from the Lord*
> *Who heav'n and earth hath made.)*

And with his departure, something passed from the little church in Elphin that has never been replaced. It was the close of an era.

The beginning of my student life marked the end of my home life in Elphin. But the spell that it cast upon me in my boyhood never lifted. Some years after I left, and during my Greenock ministry, I picked up a morning paper − *The Bulletin* − and found an article in it which read like this:

ELPHIN

"There is really a place called Elphin on the map of Scotland. Stranger still, it is not unworthy of its charming and fantastic name. You climb out of Strath Oykell and cross a wide vast of greenish-brown bent, greenish-gold perhaps in the oblique light of evening. Suddenly something is there beyond it that was not there before, something that makes you gasp – the incredible blue cone of Suilven. Then on the right, Ben More Assynt heaves into view.

"You come to a sign-post which offers one of the most distracting choices in all Scotland. 'Ullapool 18 miles' says one arm; 'Lochinver 19 miles' says the other. If you choose the first, you turn sharp left, cross a bridge, and zig-zag upwards till you are high on a hill-side above three or four sprawling lochs. You take a hairpin bend (more than one perhaps), negotiate an iron gate or so, and you are in Elphin.

"It is what geography calls an alp — an upland pasture isolated by barren hills. It is an Alpen-wiese almost, a meadow among hills. You could wade knee-deep in the flowers – creamy meadow-sweet, purple vetch and yellow vetch, red-purple knapweed, and blue-purple scabious.

"The houses are situated beside the road or perched in little hillocks above it. Some of them must command some of the most striking views in all Scotland – Suilven and Canisp rising precipitous above their gleaming lochs.

"The narrow road runs round the valley. You cannot see how it is ever to get out, the end of the world seems so obviously in sight. But it finds a shelf, just wide enough for one car and, following that, between earth and heaven, between a steep, heathery brae and a frowning cornice of rock, which breaks down in waves of scree to the very roadside, you leave Elphin behind."

Leave Elphin behind! But do you? Nay, but the nameless writer's speech betrayeth him! A man who could write like that shows that, even in the passing, he had taken something unforgettable with him when he went on his way.

And so did I. A treasury of memories so rich, so precious, so abidingly stimulating, that my debt to the land of my youth must ever remain undischarged.

> *If thee Jerus'lem I forget*
> *Skill part from my right hand.*

7: Renewing Connections

The London to which I returned in 1919 was very different from the city of my boyhood. My early impressions, of course, had not been deep, and the passing years had blurred them. But the comparison that the older people were constantly making between pre-War and post-War London helped to bring back, and set in sharper focus, an order of things that I had almost forgotten, and relate it to the new situation which had emerged.

The struggle for survival which had marked the 1914-18 War period had sharpened the genius of the embattled nations as they pitted their wits against each other in their laboratories and factories and struggled for the mastery, and it was clear that our country would never be the same again. The brave promises about producing "a country fit for heroes to live in" were showing little sign of being fulfilled. The nation was discovering that it was easier to win the war than win the peace. The representatives of the nations who were planning the brave new world that men were looking for had got on to wrong lines.

A clever cartoon appeared in an American magazine around this time. A planning committee which had been entrusted with the preparation of the agenda for one of the great peace conferences of those days had run into difficulty at the very outset as to whether the sessions of Conference should be opened with an act of worship.

The cartoonist hit off the situation neatly. His drawing represented a large hand holding a small globe, upon which rested a small table with a number of small men seated around it. But one chair was vacant, and that was what the discussion was all about. The caption said simply:

Shall we invite Him in?

And because men are still giving the wrong answer the world's turmoil continues. For *"except the Lord build the house, they labour in vain that build it..."*

An arrogant humanism was taking over, and the Churches, enfeebled by the rationalistic philosophy that had infiltrated so many of the theological colleges in the pre-war years appeared to have lost the confidence and respect of the masses. The dearly-loved

Gospel message of earlier times was at a discount. The godly remnant were expressing their feelings in the lamentation of the Covenanter woman of earlier times:

> *There's nae Gospel noo, lassie,*
> *There's nae Covenant blood,*
> *There's nae altar noo, lassie,*
> *There's nae Lamb o' God.*
>
> *Folks dinna want the Cross,*
> *lassie,*
> *They've cutten doon the tree,*
> *And naebody believes in't*
> *But fules like you and me.*

But things were not as bad as they seemed; they never are. For wherever the evangel of the Cross was faithfully preached, proof was not lacking that the message of Christ and Him crucified was still "the power of God unto salvation to every one that believeth."

There was no Free Church of Scotland congregation in London in those days, so I considered the different places where one might expect to find good preaching. The Metropolitan Tabernacle was an early choice. The great ministry of C.H. Spurgeon had closed thirty years before, and the congregation that used to crowd the vast auditorium had melted away. The church fabric itself had been largely destroyed by fire shortly after Spurgeon's death, but had been re-built, and was under the ministry of H.Tydeman Chilvers. His message was fully worthy of Spurgeon's pulpit, but by then, there were scarcely as many hundreds in the pews as there had been thousands in Spurgeon's hey-day.

It is never easy to succeed to the pulpit of a celebrity. Dr. Joseph Parker's old church, the City Temple, had by then as its pastor Dr. F.W. Norwood but, again, the attendances had dwindled to mediocrity. Westminster Chapel, under the ministry of Dr. Campbell Morgan, was still thriving, but it was his week-night Bible Class that, for the most part, I attended. Dr. J. Stuart Holden was in Portman Square, and attracting large congregations. Some time afterwards we had him, and Campbell Morgan in Edinburgh for a students' campaign and they took well. A journalist who covered some of their meetings provided a comparison of them that I found interesting. He quotes from a letter which appeared in the *Monthly Evangel* from a lady who was present at one of the meetings. She tells that as she waited for the meeting to begin, a working-man who was sitting in front of her was joined by an acquaintance, when the following conversation took place.

"I havena seen ye here afore."

"No, I couldna get afore. I'm in frae the country."

"Then ye'll no' hae heard Dr. Morgan, man, but ye must hear him, he's gran'. But (softening his voice and looking along the platform at Dr. Holden) he's an awfu' sweet, gracious soul this. Aye he'll min' ye o' the Maister. Jist."'

Dr. Stuart Holden gave a fine address to a students' gathering in the Free Church College during that visit, an address that I have cause to remember. Professor Maclean, who presided, had asked me, in view of my earlier contacts with Dr. Holden, to be ready with a word of thanks to him at the end of the meeting. But Dr. Holden, in a lighter moment at the beginning of his address, referred to something that a speaker had said about himself at a recent meeting in England — something embarrassing in substance and in length — with the result that when I was called upon to propose the vote of thanks I did so with almost telegraphic brevity, which, it would seem was not in character. Dr. Maclean looked at me with some surprise and then , turning to Dr. Holden, remarked with mock severity, "It was that story of yours that did it. You cramped his style." It was my turn to be embarrassed.

Dr. Stuart Holden and Rev. George Mackay of Fearn Free Church were firm friends and lost no opportunity of getting together. Stuart Holden used often to holiday in Inverness-shire, and on one of these occasions he motored to Fearn on Sabbath to hear his friend preach. When they met, Mr. Mackay insisted that his visitor must preach. Dr. Holden's protestations of unreadiness were to no avail. As a last resort he urged the unseemliness of his appearing in a Presbyterian pulpit in holiday attire. "Oh, we shall soon see to that," replied Mr. Mackay and half-propelling him into his vestry he produced his Moderatorial robe (he had recently presided over the General Assembly) and proceeded to drape it over his visitor's shoulders. Standing back and casting an appraising eye over the Doctor, he then remarked, "There now, nobody could ever tell that you are an Episcopalian!" Ever afterwards Mr. Mackay maintained that the best sermon he ever heard from the Doctor was the one he preached in Fearn Free Church in a Presbyterian vestment!

Dr. F.B. Meyer of Christ Church was another of the London preachers I used to hear in my student days. His quiet dignity and sustained serenity never failed to impress, although he himself was quite unaware of these qualities. His books read well, even in this fastidious age, and they continue to command a wide circulation throughout the English-speaking world.

The last time I heard Dr. Meyer speak was in Toronto, in 1927. It was a meeting for young people in particular, and the large audience bore no trace of what, in present-day parlance, we refer to as "the generation gap". Dr. Meyer was an old man by that time, unable to stand while preaching, and using a high stool. But his voice had lost nothing of its musicality and range.

I still recall an illustration that he used towards the end of his address. He had been urging the practice of prayerful Bible-reading, and testifying to the benefit that he himself had derived from doing so.

Just a few days before then, he said, he had broken his journey at a certain railway-junction in the United States and, as he awaited the arrival of the train that was to take him the relatively short journey to a town where he was to preach in the passing, he checked his train times on a long railway-folder that he carried in a coat-pocket. He then took out his Bible to look up a reference. Having done so, he was about to return the Bible to his pocket when an American gentleman who was sitting beside him in the waiting-room said, "Sir, would you mind giving me, in just a few words, your reason for trusting that Book as you evidently do? I am quite serious."

There was no time for a lengthy answer, for the train was almost due. The time-table that was still in his hand gave him an idea.

"Do you see this folder?" he asked. "I got it in New York when I set out on this journey. I have been consulting it all along the way, and have found it thoroughly reliable. There is not much of the journey left. Can you suggest any reason why, having found it entirely accurate hitherto, I should begin to doubt it for the short distance that remains?"

"Well, I guess not, Sir; but I was really talking about the Bible."

"Yes," said Dr. Meyer, "and I am just coming to that. You see this Bible? From early life, I have taken it as my guide through all the bewildering changes of life. It has been a lamp to my feet and a light to my path. I am now an old man, and the end of my journey is in sight. Having found the Bible so completely trustworthy throughout a long life can you suggest any reason why I should not trust it now?"

"I guess not, Sir," replied the American, "and I thank you for your answer. It is just what I needed."

Dr. Meyer had a responsive audience as he applied his parable that evening, and urged his young audience to trust God and follow the guidance of His word all their days.

But of all the prominent Non-Conformist preachers in London at that time there was not one who drew me as strongly as did Dr. Dinsdale T. Young.

A man of portly build and decidedly impressive appearance, the vast Westminster Hall seemed to have been built for him, and his rich, sonorous voice carried to its remotest corners. Dinsdale T. Young belonged to an age when oratory was of much account, and his arresting Johnsonian style made its own contribution to the effectiveness of his preaching. I still have several volumes of his sermons on my shelves, but even the best of them gives but little impression of the power of his spoken word. As a professed Calvinist he was a *rara avis* among Methodists, and he frequently confessed his indebtedness to Scottish preachers of the Reformed school. "I have many of their books on my shelves," I once heard him say, "and special favourites such as Rutherford's *Letters* and M'Cheyne's *Sermons* are not on my shelves simply because they are usually on my desk."

My last meeting with Dr. Dinsdale Young was at the service held in Finnieston Church, Glasgow, to celebrate the ministerial jubilee of his friend, Dr. David M. M'Intyre – then Principal of the Bible Training Institute, Glasgow. I had been doing the Protestant Institute Lectures in Edinburgh and Glasgow that session, and had requested Dr. M'Intyre to preside at my opening lecture in Glasgow and, knowing my admiration for Dinsdale Young, he had invited me to his jubilee celebrations which were to be held later in the year. Dr. Young was still hale and hearty, and his address was fully worthy of the occasion.

My years in Sutherland had drawn, and warmly attached me, to the ethos of the Free Church of Scotland, and had given me such an esteem of Reformed teaching that nothing else would now satisfy me. With no Free Church congregation in London at that juncture, the Free Church ministers who came from time to time to conduct the Gaelic services, held quarterly in Crown Court Church, were welcome visitors and I invariably enjoyed their fellowship and benefited from their preaching.

The time came when, hearing that the Free Presbyterians had a mission hall in the vicinity of Victoria Station, with services on Sabbath and a prayer meeting on a week-day evening, I set out one evening to see if I could find it. I looked at a number of likely places but drew a blank. I chanced, however, to see a soberly clad gentleman who, I impulsively decided, must be either a Free Presbyterian missionary or a Jewish Rabbi! On this slim clue, I accosted him and asked if, by any chance, he knew of a hall in this vicinity where a small company of Scottish Free Presbyterians were wont to meet for religious services. The good man positively beamed at me in mingled surprise and pleasure, and told me that he was just on his way there himself to conduct the weekly prayer-meeting. He turned out to be the missionary in charge at the time – a Mr. Angus Macrae whose nephew, the Rev. Murdoch Macrae M.A., was soon to become one of my closest friends and fellow-students, and the highly esteemed minister of Kinloch, Lewis.

The London Free Presbyterians had no minister at that time, nor for some years after, but I greatly appreciated the warm-hearted, spiritual, preaching of Angus Macrae, as also that of John MacKay who came after him.

A Gaelic sermon in cosmopolitan and polyglot London was always a treat not to be missed. But when, on returning to Scotland to study for the ministry I was able to revert to a more normal church life and attach myself to a well-established Free Church congregation which provided not only two English services every Sabbath, but also the luxury of a Gaelic service in addition, I felt the lines were indeed fallen to me in pleasant places.

Especially when the preacher was Alexander Stewart.

8: In Scotland Again

I well remember the first service that I attended in Free St. Columba's, Edinburgh. The Rev. Donald Maclean had been the first minister there after the upheaval of the 1900 Church Union, but he had left the pastorate in 1918 on being appointed by the General Assembly as Highland Secretary of the Supply Committee. In 1920 he became Professor of Church History and Church Principles in the Free Church College, in succession to Professor Colin Bannatyne, who retired in that year.

The original Free St. Columba's Church in Cambridge Street had been allocated to the United Free Church, while the former Free St. John's Church was assigned to the Free Church to serve the dual purpose of a church for the dispossessed St. Columba's congregation, and an Assembly Hall for the denomination. The Martyrs' Church on George IV Bridge, which had been a Reformed Presbyterian Church under the ministry of Dr. W.H. Goold, had joined the Free Church in 1876, and now received into its membership the dispossessed Free St. John's people.

Meanwhile, Rev. Alexander Stewart of the Free Presbyterian Church in Edinburgh, with the majority of his congregation, had been received into the Free Church under the name Fountainbridge Free Church.

When therefore the Rev. Donald Maclean became Highland Secretary in 1918 St. Columba's and Fountainbridge united under the ministry of Rev. Alexander Stewart. Designated St. Columba-Fountainbridge Free Church to begin with, the new name was found to be cumbersome and misleading, for newcomers and visitors tended to look for the building in Fountainbridge instead of the Lawnmarket.

This then was the congregation of which I became a member in 1921.

To sit under the ministry of Dr. Stewart (as he became in 1926) was a rare privilege. A man of wide culture and deep spiritual insight, he was one of the best expository preachers I have ever known. He had a fine gift of communication, both by voice and pen. His literary gifts were recognised by the Church when, in 1906, he was appointed Editor of *The Instructor*, which was founded in that year. In 1917 he succeeded Archibald MacNeilage as the Editor of the *Monthly Record*, the denominational magazine of the Free Church of Scotland.

Perhaps the Bible-class conducted by Dr. Stewart and held after the Sabbath evening service was, to the students and other young people in the congregation, the best congregational event in the round of the week, for he was a born teacher. Though the class was designed primarily for young people, the older folk were told that they might wait on too if they so desired. And many did. The annual social meeting, almost always held in the Protestant Institute Hall on a suitable week-night, was a very special occasion, when distinguished men from various walks of life were engaged as visiting speakers.

I recall one fine address by Lord Wark, the eminent jurist, at one of these meetings. Lord Wark and Dr. Stewart had become acquainted during holidays in the Isle of Arran. Dr. Stewart had been advised, on medical grounds, to take up golf as a suitable open-air recreation, and Lord Wark was a keen exponent of the game — a fact to which Dr. Stewart made facetious reference in introducing him to the audience. They had all heard, he said, about Lord Wark, for he was a man of many interests and activities. He had acquired fame in his own profession, first at the Bar, and then on the Bench. "But" continued Dr. Stewart, "I have never heard him at the Bar, nor on the Bench; but I have heard him in a Bunker, and he acquitted himself in every way as a Christian gentleman."

And with that he called upon Lord Wark to address the company. This he did, cleverly linking his opening words with Dr. Stewart's introduction.

He had heard of Dr. Stewart, he said, as an excellent Preacher, and a skilful Pleader in the Assembly. "But", he continued, "I have never heard him from the Pulpit, nor have I heard him from the Platform; but I *have* heard him in a Bunker, *and he impressed me as a model of Christian resignation!*"

And having given Dr. Stewart a Roland for his Oliver, he launched into a gripping address on Christian Citizenship.

Church History came alive for me in those early years in St. Columba's. Dr. Thomas Guthrie's famous pulpit, copied from a design that he had seen somewhere on the Continent, was a constant reminder of his virtual ejection from the Establishment in 1843 when Parliament finally dismissed the Church's just plea for the restoration of her spiritual independence. And his plaque, now back in the vestibule of the Church after its removal by the United Free Church to Martyrs and St. John's United Free Church, is a symbol in stone of the post-1900 Free Church's claim to be the authentic Free Church of Scotland in direct descent from the Disruption Fathers.

But still more interesting to me were the prominent Churchmen I could pick out in the congregation as I looked around the Church on that unforgettable Sabbath morning. There was Professor Donald Maclean, a former minister of the congregation, and Professor J. Kennedy Cameron, one of the first Professors in the reconstituted Free Church College. In a seat flanking the pulpit was the massive figure of Professor John R. Mackay, whom I had already met at a Communion service in Coigach after he had joined the Free Church from the Free Presbyterian Church in 1918. And last but not least there was Sir James Simpson, the brilliant lawyer who had done so much to help the Free Church retain its heritage in the stirring events at the beginning of the century.

Altogether it was an exciting morning which reached its climax in a gripping sermon on the Parable of the Lost Sheep, preached by Mr. Stewart.

Of the pulpit celebrities of other denominations in Edinburgh I saw but little in my student days. There were two main reasons for this. First, the Free Church had still a large number of vacant pulpits at the time, thus necessitating a great deal of "supply" work from the students and, second, I was not inclined to ecclesiastical vagrancy, and wanted to hear my own minister as much as I could.

Dr. James Black was at the height of his popularity in United Free St. George's at the time, and I used to see the queueing crowds waiting for admission, as I cycled along Shandwick Place on my way to St. Columba's of a Sabbath morning. James Black's brother, Hugh, had been colleague in St. George's with Dr. Alexander Whyte in earlier years, but had gone to New York. The two men were so utterly unlike that they got on well together. Whyte could be a prophet of judgment when the mood was on him, and sinners came limply through his hands. But Black took a more flattering view of human nature, so the saying became current that people went to St. George's to be black-balled by Dr. Whyte, and then to be whitewashed by Dr. Black.

I heard Dr. James Black twice; once in his own Church, and again at a university service, but I was more impressed by his dramatic style than by the doctrinal content of his sermons.

Dr. James MacGregor was then in nearby St. Cuthbert's and had won widespread acclaim as a preacher. A deformed, dwarfish man, his bodily presence was indeed weak, but his "speech" was certainly not "contemptible". He could capture an audience and hold it for so long as it pleased him. He liked to see distinguished people in his congregation and he wanted everybody to know they were there. So he told the Almighty in his prayers that they were present and invoked His blessing upon them.

He was a stickler for ceremony, and could needle his visiting preachers by his emphasis on protocol. He had engaged Dr. A.K.H. Boyd of St. Andrews for the re-dedication service after St. Cuthbert's had been enlarged and refurbished during his ministry. As the day for the service drew near he kept prodding Boyd with questions and suggestions until he provoked him to mischievous retaliation. The opportunity came when MacGregor wrote to him to ask for a note of the text that he planned to take at the re-dedication service. Back went a letter which said, "I have been thinking that nothing could be more appropriate than, 'I will pull down my barns and build greater!' "

It took "wee MacGregor", as he was familiarly known, a moment or two to realise that his leg was being pulled!

Dr. Maclean Watt was then at St. Stephen's. I heard him once, but not in his own Church. I came to know him in his retirement for, when he was in Edinburgh over the weekend, he sometimes dropped in on us in St. Columba's.

As a Royal Chaplain he was a great favourite with King George VI and the Queen Mother. On one occasion during a visit to Balmoral he disclosed to the Queen that, for long spells, he lived alone in a former lighthouse on a little island in Loch Carron.

"But how do you do for cooking?" asked the Queen.

As he was telling her, the King entered the room, and the Queen brought him into the conversation. "Dr. Maclean Watt," she said, "has just been telling me that sometimes he lives alone in a now-disused lighthouse on a small island and, not only that; he does his own cooking. Isn't that wonderful?"

"Oh, Ma'am, I can tell you something more wonderful than that. I *eat* it too!"

Maclean Watt was so richly endowed by the Muses that his very prose was poetry.

The minister of Charlotte Chapel (Baptist) in those years was Dr. W. Graham Scroggie. I went twice to hear him, and once, as President of the Free Church Students' Association, I had him along to the College to address the Annual Reunion. He rose excellently to the occasion and was much appreciated.

9: Under the Yoke

My introduction to the pulpit was unplanned and quite unexpected, and Rev. Angus Mackay of Kingussie had much to do with it.

During the later period of my studies in London I was becoming increasingly aware of a change in my attitude toward the ministry of the Gospel. Given a sense of call to the work I felt that nothing else would matter. Difficult adjustments would have to be made, but these could be faced with faith and courage. But the question was — was I *called*? How could I know? I was not looking for visions or audible voices from the Lord, although I had no difficulty in accepting that, if He were so minded, He might choose to communicate with people today in those ways just as He had done in former times. But I *did* long for guidance. The prayer of the Psalmist was often in my heart, "Shew me thy ways, O Lord; teach me thy paths. Lead me in thy truth, and teach me."

But the time had come for me to make my decision, and I used a visit to Elphin for the purpose. The details of the day that I set apart specially for this event need not be told; sufficient to say that by the time I returned home in the late afternoon I had made up my mind that guidance regarding the ministry was not as clear as I deemed necessary for such an important decision. Accordingly, I assumed it to be my duty to abandon all thought of it and return to London.

Just as I neared the house I met our local postman and collected our mail from him. One item was a small package addressed to me — obviously a book — but there was nothing to disclose the identity of the sender. I turned to the back pages of the book to see if any message had been inserted there; but there was nothing. The title of the book was *The Almost Christian*, and the author, Matthew Mead, one of the lesser-known Puritans. How the book came to be sent to me I was quite unaware until some time afterwards, but while looking for a clue, my eyes fell upon words which , as I read, seemed to take fire and to have a special bearing on my own circumstances at the time.

But it might be better to revert to Rev. Angus Mackay at this point.

In the Preface to his booklet *A Goodly Heritage*, where he acknowledges the help of friends in its production, he writes:

"In the year 1919 my son, Rev. John Calvin Mackay M.A., who was in that year an Examiner under the Welfare of Youth Scheme of the Free Church of Scotland, showed me the entry to which he had awarded the first prize in the Essay Competition. The subject was, *'Why I belong to the Free Church of Scotland.'* The Essay seemed more like the product of a theological student than of a schoolboy, and, on reading it, I immediately wrote to Mr. Duncan MacRae, an elder of the Free Church in the district in Sutherland where the successful competitor was then residing, expressing the conviction that the youthful essayist would yet be a minister of the Gospel. A reply came from the boy himself. He declared that nothing in the world would give him greater joy than to be a Free Church minister if he thought he was called to the work, but he had a dread of being a blind leader of the blind.

"A few years passed, and the young student returned from Scotland to his home in London. While thinking of him on one occasion, I went back in imagination to the home of a Mr. Donald MacKay, where I had lodged while teaching in a public school at Braemar, Ontario, in 1873, where I was treated as a member of the family though charged only $1.25 per week! I recalled my host's interest in a book by Matthew Mead, *Almost a Christian*, and how at times he used to read a sentence or two aloud to the family circle, with the remark, 'This is very searching!' These thoughts led me to send my own copy of that old book to the student in London.

"Some time afterwards I received a letter from him to say that in opening the book at random when it came to his hand, the first sentence which he read was, 'My brethren, remember this; slighted convictions are the worst death-bed companions. There are two things especially, which above all others, make a death-bed very uncomfortable: 1. Purposes and promises not performed; 2. Convictions slighted and not improved.' It was a word in season, and marked the turning-point in his life."

The effect of my encounter with Matthew Mead was indeed, as my old friend says, to mark the turning point in my life in the respect that I no longer resisted (as I now realised I had been doing) the call to the ministry. God, as I now believed, was rebuking my vacillations, and cautioning me against continuing in them. Whatever the future might hold, Christ's yoke in the ministry of His Church must be upon my shoulder, and I was well content that it should be so.

I want to make another reference to Matthew Mead before I leave the subject. During my theological course in the Free Church

College, I was sitting one day with Professor J.R. Mackay in his retiring-room discussing the renewed interest in Puritan teaching that was beginning to reveal itself, when he asked which of the Puritans was my favourite.

"Favourite! I'm not sure I can answer that," I replied, "But the one who influenced me most at a particular time in my life was undoubtedly Matthew Mead, with his *Almost Christian.*"

Dr. Mackay smiled reminiscently. "I was the same," he said. "When I first went to University there were just two religious books that I took with me, along with my Bible; and they were Matthew Mead's *Almost Christian* and Samuel Rutherford's *Letters.* I used to read them together, reading Mead until he scarified me, and then turning to Rutherford for comfort. But they went well together."

I was less cautious. I used to stay with Mead until he left me limp and comfortless. What a solace it would have been in those moments to have had some such word from Rutherford as he wrote to Marion MacNaught in one of his incomparable Letters, "Send a heavy heart up to Christ, it shall be welcome."

My letter to Rev. Angus Mackay, to which he refers in the preface to his booklet from which I have quoted, was really written by me at Duncan MacRae's urgent request, for, as I have already mentioned, in his latter years, owing to the paralysis in his right arm, he was no longer able to write. But from that time my contacts with Mr. Mackay became more personal, and led to an invitation to spend a few days in Kingussie manse. And there, he almost literally press gangcd me into the pulpit. There was a Gaelic service in Newtonmore in those days and he suggested to me that I take it. I was aghast at the very thought, and protested that I had never as yet attempted to preach, and, in any case, that I should require longer time for preparation — especially as the service was to be in Gaelic. But it was all to no purpose, and on the following afternoon we were on our bicycles making for Newtonmore Church.

To preach a first sermon in the presence of a minister was a big enough ordeal by itself, but it almost became a trial by fire. For I had scarcely begun my sermon when there was a loud report at my left ear, caused, fortunately, by nothing more sinister than the shattering of the glass funnel of a paraffin lamp!

My text, I remember, was the appeal of the Philippian Jailer, "*Sirs, what must I do to be saved?*", and Paul's answer, "*Believe on the Lord Jesus Christ, and thou shalt be saved.*" It articulates man's greatest need. It expresses God's greatest mercy.

To say the least, my mood after my first attempt at preaching was not self-congratulatory, and I would fain have gone into hiding for the rest of the day. But when my kind host proposed that I share the evening service at Kingussie with him I did not demur, but qualified my concurrence with the proviso that I should not be required to do more than read a chapter or take a prayer. In the event, I did both. Probably, Mr. Mackay had sensed my feelings and had decided that the best way to treat a rather shaken young recruit was to send him back into the fray but in a less daunting role. At all events, it must have been sound psychology, for before the week was out I actually *volunteered* to take a service which he had arranged at Insh so as to spare him the strain of negotiating those roads which, by this time, were blocked with drifted snow. The frost was so keen however that the snow was frozen hard and not too difficult to traverse. The moon was full, the night still and bright, and the people of Insh friendly and kind. The complete solitude suited me; for I had much to think about. That night, at that little meeting in the snow-girt cottage I thought I sensed an extra Presence – and I was reminded that the Great Commissioner who had said "GO – " had also said "LO...*I am with you alway.*" And I was glad.

I was where I wanted to be – under His yoke. And for the present, nothing else mattered.

On reflection, I realise that the frequent demands made upon us, as students, for weekend preaching must have been detrimental to our academic work. The Church itself seemed rather ambivalent in the matter. The Training of the Ministry Committee tended to frown on preaching engagements for students except in vacations, but, when we tried to go by this plan, the "Supply" Committee would urge us, in view of the special needs of the Church at the time, to make ourselves as fully available as possible for work among the pastorless congregations.

Several of the Free Church congregations in Kintyre were vacant at the time and were particularly inaccessible. To get to Lochgilphead from Edinburgh, for example, meant that the student had to go to Glasgow on Friday night in order to connect with the Saturday 8.20 a.m. train for Gourock where he boarded the MacBrayne steamer for Ardrishaig. The remaining two miles, or so, of the journey were done in Victorian luxury, in a four-wheeled passenger coach drawn by two horses. That, quite definitely, was the bit I liked most. We arrived in early afternoon and did not get away again until around noon on Monday, arriving back in Edinburgh around 10 p.m. *when the ship managed to keep her connections!*

"You poor students," gushed a dear old Lochgilphead lady, "we are so sorry for you, having to come all this way at the end of a busy week in College, to preach to us. But we *do* enjoy having you."

Now, the student addressed, as it happened, was a native Gaelic speaker with, at the time, a poor English vocabulary and only a dim idea of the meaning of the words which it contained. "Ah, yes," he responded, in tones heavy with self-pity, "it is true that Free Church students are very *circumcised*. But we enjoy coming."

Fortunately, the lady's vocabulary was limited also!

But, "circumscribed" as we were, we tried to meet the requests made to us. And there were compensations. To begin with, what could be better for our health then to get out of the city at weekends, and enjoy the hospitality of the kind friends who lodged in the various delectable places to which we were sent? The journeys were often long and tedious, but the fresh breezes of the Firth of Clyde and Loch Fyne, and the sharp winds of the Grampians whetted our appetites for the "feast of fat things" at the journey's end. More than that, these excursions gave us an excellent training for days to come. For it is one thing to be taught the art of preaching in a College classroom, and quite another to practise it in the presence of a congregation assembled for the worship of God. And the comments of the good elders who cared enough for the young preacher to suggest to him ways in which he could make his message more effective were sometimes of more value than the classroom hints that related to a discourse prescribed as a College exercise.

I well remember an experience that befell me in this connection in my very early days as a preacher. I had been sent to Tain for a weekend, before ever the small post-1900 congregation had grown to the status of a regular pastorate. The church building, in those days, was a small, unpretentious corrugated-iron structure, and the low pulpit and pews were just too close to suit the composure of the occupants of either. Added to that, there sat right in my line of vision a gentleman of distinctly patrician appearance, who busied himself in note-taking during the service. He was obviously a man of quality, and I found myself wishing he had gone elsewhere that morning. Those keen, penetrating glances and that busy yellow pencil left me uncomfortable. But he was waiting for me when I came out from the vestry, and greeted me with an affability that set me at ease. He spoke with kind appreciation of the address I had just given, and then added, "I wonder if you would be good enough to let an old man who has done a bit of preaching himself speak a few words of counsel to you?"

I begged him, please, to do so; and there, just outside the vestry door, I was given the most kindly, helpful and comprehensive criticism that I had ever listened to. Principally, it concerned my use of words. From his notes, he selected some polysyllabic words I had used and then suggested some simple synonyms that would have conveyed my meaning far more readily to the greater part of my audience. A large part of the appeal of C.H.Spurgeon, he maintained, lay in his studied simplicity.

I thanked him for his thoughtfulness in waiting to speak to me, and assured him that I would always bear in mind his wise counsels. I met him once or twice in after years and always benefited from his fellowship. He was Commander Wolfe Murray, a Christian gentleman who was well known in many parts of the country as a zealous Christian worker and a tireless preacher.

Perhaps my most disconcerting experience of preaching before unrecognised notables in student days was in Lairg. I had gone there to stand-in for the minister there — the Rev. J. Mackay Maclennan M.A., who was on a visit to Canada.

When I entered the Lairg pulpit that morning my eyes almost immediately fell on two gentlemen in clerical dress who were sitting well back in the centre of the church.

Who were they? In my attempts at identification I confined myself to the Free Church of Scotland, and one of the visitors looked uncommonly like a well-known minister who was reputed to regard student preachers as a sad necessity of the times! But when the suspect raised his hand and I saw the glint of a massive gold ring on one of his fingers, comfort and courage returned, for the minister whose presence I had dreaded would certainly not be seen wearing a gold ring!

A week passed before I discovered who the visiting clerics were — none other than Dr. Randall Davidson, Archbishop of Canterbury; and Dr. Winnington Ingram, Bishop of London. They were on a short holiday in Lairg at the time. They had been kind enough the following day to enquire after me with a view to inviting me to dinner at their hotel, but were informed that I had left the village by an early train on the Monday morning. So I never discovered what the Archbishop thought of my sermon!

It was better so!

Dr. Davidson was actually interested in the Free Church of Scotland, and in the stormy sequel to the 1900 Church Union, had offered his services as a mediator between the disputing parties. It was kindly meant, but it was high optimism to expect that estranged

Scottish Presbyterians would regard with favour a proposal —
however well-motivated — that the Archbishop of Canterbury
should act as a placator between them. Shades of William Laud!

Randall Davidson had a reputation as an ecclesiastical trouble-
shooter, and had given rise to a limerick in this connection. A bitter
controversy had broken out in the mission-field between two
missionary bishops and the case had been referred to Davidson for
arbitration.

The limerick runs:

> A bishop, a Zanzibarbarian
> Suspected some bishops were Arian.
> So he went up to Randall,
> for bell, book and candle,
> But Randall, well Randall's a wary 'un.

10: Assisting in Glasgow

For two years of my student life I spent most of my weekends and holidays in Glasgow as student-assistant in Hope Street Free Church — an appointment that brought me into contact with one of the most interesting Churchmen I have ever known. I refer to Dr. James Duff McCulloch, the Senior Minister of Hope Street Free Church. By then, Dr. McCulloch had retired from the active ministry of the pastorate, and Rev. John Macleod O.B.E. had been inducted as his Colleague and Successor. The partnership was a happy one.

In 1926 Mr. Macleod spent some months in Canada, ministering to the Gaelic-speaking emigrants who, under pressure of economic conditions at home, had sought employment in the Dominion. Several ministers had promised to help with the Sabbath services, and I continued in the normal duties of assistantship, with such additional ones as might arise in the minister's absence.

By that time Dr. McCulloch was almost completely blind, and could not go out of doors unaccompanied. Members of his own family, with the assistance of friends, used to bring him to the various meetings that he wished to attend from time to time. One of these, however, was a Gaelic prayer-meeting held on Monday evenings, and since none of the McCulloch family understood the language, it became my privilege to call for him and bring him home again.

It was then that my evening really began. Dr. McCulloch was not an early bedder and, cut off as he was from his treasured books, he sometimes felt the evening long if he had no one to speak with. Even a raw student was welcome!

Now I had recently read David Brown's *In the Pulpit and at the Communion Table*, a compilation of sermons and addresses by Dr. John Duncan, better known as "Rabbi Duncan". The book contained also some reminiscences of the "Rabbi" contributed by ministers who had been his students — James Duff McCulloch among them. I was thrilled! I had previously read Dr. Moody Stuart's *Recollections of John Duncan LL.D.*, and had completely fallen under the "Rabbi's" spell. And here I was, in close touch with one of his students!

In those Monday evening chats I often contrived ways of bringing in a reference to the "Rabbi" by way of priming, and it seldom failed; for Dr. McCulloch's veneration for his old teacher had never waned. He added to my stock of amusing stories relating to the "Rabbi's" absent-mindedness, but these were not the memories that he loved most to recall.

He spoke one evening of Dr. Duncan's moods of depression, recalling, in particular, a morning when he came into the classroom the very embodiment of dejection. It was evident to those who knew him that he was in the arena fighting, as it seemed, a losing battle. The class stood for the short prayer with which it was customary to begin, but the words were slow to come.

The young men agonised in sympathy with their master, but still the heavens were as brass and the earth as iron. Then, suddenly, a gleam of light seemed to flit over the Professor's face. The tension was yielding. The words were coming more fluently. The petitioner had obviously won through to the Throne of Grace and was having an audience of the King. And then the bell signalled the end of the hour.

"We got no Hebrew that day," recalled Dr. McCulloch, "but I do not expect to hear such exalted language again on this side of heaven." And, as he spoke, there was a dawning of light as of another world upon his own face.

James D. McCulloch had passed through the New College while it was still at the height of its fame as a stronghold of Reformed Evangelicalism and a centre of learning. Truly, there were giants in the earth in those days, and their influence was clearly evident in many of their students. James D. McCulloch was one of them. He was just seven years of age when the Disruption took place, but the struggle between Church and State that was agitating Scotland at the time gripped his interest from boyhood. His first charge was Latheron, in Caithness, where he became Colleague and Successor to Rev. George Davidson, who had "come out" at the Disruption. Mr. McCulloch married Mr. Davidson's daughter Isabella, and one of their sons, Andrew, a loyal son of the Church, came to the help of the Free Church as her first General Treasurer after the crippling crisis of 1900.

Wisdom and prudence marked Mr. McCulloch from the very beginning of his ministry. Latheron was rent by the Separatist movement before he went there, and Mr. Davidson had not gone out of his way to regain the dissenters. Their leader, a man of undoubted piety, although of rather rash disposition, was Donald Grant, the local teacher, who used his school-room as a place of public worship for the Separatists, on the Lord's Day. Between Mr. Davidson and Donald Grant there was no attempt at Christian co-operation; the most they could achieve was Christian avoidance. They kept out of each other's way.

When Mr. McCulloch came to the parish, however, he laid himself out to cultivate the friendship of the old Separatist leader. In his pastoral rounds he never omitted to visit Donald Grant, and a firm friendship gradually grew up between them. Mr. Davidson had always refused to baptise the children of non-churchgoing parents with whom he classed the families who had broken away from the Church and were attending the Separatist meetings. Mr. McCulloch was less rigid in this respect and, other things being in order, he baptised the children of Separatist parents who made and maintained a "credible profession."

The Rev. George Sutherland of Bruan, who wrote a short biography of Donald Grant, tells how Donald made it known that "he was now convinced that he did wrong in standing out from the Church and in maintaining separate services at church hours," and that he would "gladly go to the Free Church at Latheron on the Communion Sabbath if the state of his health would allow him."

As it happened his health deteriorated so rapidly that this intention was never realised. But something even more significant happened. Mr. McCulloch intimated one Sabbath morning in the Latheron Church that the evening service would be held by him in Donald Grant's meeting-house in Boultach.

That meeting marked the beginning of better things in the parish, and Separatism soon became a thing of the past.

Dr. McCulloch died in 1926 at the ripe age of 90, having retained the Principalship of the College to the end. The entire College personnel, Professors and students, attended the funeral service in Hope Street Free Church, Glasgow, and the vast and representative gathering which assembled there, and later followed the fallen standard-bearer to his burial, bore impressive witness not only to the place that he had occupied in the life of the Church at large, but to the impression that his ministry had made upon the city.

A story once told me about him by his co-presbyter in Glasgow, Rev. John Macleod, of Duke Street Free Church, is worth repeating as an illustration of his courtesy and good sense.

During the Church Union controversy at the beginning of the century, the press one day carried a report of an attack made in the United Free Church Presbytery by Dr. Robert Howie of Govan, on

Principal McCulloch, who was recognised as a formidable opponent of the United Free Church.

The day after this report appeared, Mr. McCulloch and Mr. Macleod were walking up Renfield Street together after a church meeting, when whom should they meet but Dr. Howie, who raised his hat to his former co-presbyters in the passing. Mr. Macleod made no acknowledgment, but Mr. McCulloch courteously returned the compliment.

Mr. Macleod was disappointed. "I am surprised, Mr. McCulloch, that you should acknowledge the greeting of the man who attacked you so bitterly yesterday," he said.

"But, Mr. Macleod," came the immediate reply, "did you really think that I should let him be a better gentleman than myself?"

Feelings ran high between the two Churches in those days, and, no doubt, ungracious things were said on both sides. But none of the controversialists had less to repent of in that respect than J.D. McCulloch. He was a good swordsman but he kept his blade unsullied to the end.

While I was in Glasgow, I was too busy with studies and preaching engagements to hear many of its noted preachers. Once only did I hear Dr. George H. Morrison, who was then attracting great congregations to Wellington Church, but I was an avid reader of his sermons which issued from the presses so regularly year by year, and especially of the brief meditations so frequently exacted from him for the columns of *The British Weekly*. Several of these were published later in book form and, in the judgment of many, represented his best literary work.

Once also I heard Professor Robert Morton. The sermon had "body", but owed little to style. I got to know Dr Morton better during the years of my early ministry, and I learned to appreciate him highly. He was a tower of strength to every good cause — especially to the Scottish Reformation Society and the Lord's Day Observance Society. He might well be judged the last of the old-time Seceder Divines.

Dr. Alexander Smellie, of Carluke Original Secession Church, I also heard but once. With the fruits of his industry as a writer I was more familiar, and his justly-famed *Men of the Covenant* I still read with undiminished relish. It is a literary gem, and the writer is obviously in love with his theme.

Dr. David M'Intyre had left Finnieston Church before I went to Glasgow, and I never heard him preach, although perhaps it would be more accurate to say I never heard him do anything else. His whole life was a preaching, and his books were of the kind which are "always with grace, seasoned with salt." It was often said that he founded a new cult when he went to the Bible Training Institute as Principal. If he did, Scotland and the "regions beyond" were the better for it. If the shadow of Peter passing by brought blessing to the sick folk of Jerusalem, so the very shadow of David M. M'Intyre passing by seemed to bring blessing to his students and through them to the people among whom they later laboured.

He was one of the humblest men I ever knew. Sitting with him in his study in the B.T.I. one evening, he let slip a reference to his approaching ministerial jubilee.

"Fifty years in the ministry", I remarked, "that's a long time."

"A long time indeed", he replied, with a faint sigh, "to have done so little."

With a confusion that must have been evident, I protested that nothing could be farther from my thought than the assessment of his ministry that he had just made. I had been sitting there, I said, thinking my thoughts aloud, coveting such a ministry – so long, so varied and so fruitful — for myself. But the only response was a deprecating motion of the hand.

The last time I heard him speak was at the farewell meeting to Dr Stewart's daughter, Edith, shortly before she left for India as a missionary of the Free Church of Scotland. Edith had been one of his students in the B.T.I., and he had come to give her his parting blessing.

"That man", said a friend to me as we walked away from the meeting together, "That man gives away sovereigns as if they were farthings."

But at his jubilee meeting all that he would claim was that, "However imperfectly I have done it, I have always tried to present Christ in the glory of His Person, and in the fulness and fruitfulness of His work." And, indeed, the fragrance of the *Rose of Sharon* and the *Lily of the Valley* clings to every production of his consecrated pen.

11: Among the Exiles

My last long vacation from College was a particularly interesting one.

In those days the College Session had no summer term, but the two terms which comprised the academic year were of very much the same number of teaching days as the present three term session. In these Spartan days, when bursaries and financial grants were hard to come by, aspirants to the ministry had, in many cases, to work their way through University and College. This necessitated a more compact academic year so as to leave the students as long a free period as possible in which to earn some money for their upkeep during the ensuing session. This they did, in many cases, by obtaining appointment as teachers in country schools.

This financial stringency had been eased considerably before my time, but the academic time-table continued unchanged for some years yet.

In 1926 then, a report reached the Free Church Offices that the emigrants from the Gaelic-speaking areas of Scotland, who had settled in Toronto and its surroundings were most anxious to have a Gaelic-speaking student sent out to minister to them during the long vacation. The Foreign and Overseas Committee asked me if I would go to their aid. I agreed, but with some misgiving. My Gaelic still walked with a limp, and I wondered how I would fit in with Hebridean exiles. But the opportunity to visit Canada was not to be missed.

I went via Southampton so as to be able to visit my old home in London by the way. My booking was by the United States Lines, and it added to the thrill of the voyage that I was to travel by their ship, the *Leviathan* — then one of the largest and fastest liners afloat. We crossed to Cherbourg, where we took on a large contingent of passengers — many of them Americans. One of these, with whom I struck up an interesting friendship, was very proud of the American skills which had brought such a marvellous ship into existence, and lost no opportunity of saying so. But one day, as we were walking along a passage-way, I guided him to a plaque which I had discovered earlier in the morning and called his attention to it. It recorded that the ship, originally named the *Kaiser Wilhelm*, had been built in Hamburg, and was ceded to the United States after the First World War as part of the reparations claimed from Germany by the Allies whose merchant fleets had been so ruthlessly decimated by the German U-boats.

Perhaps it was co-incidental, but we heard less about the excellency of American shipbuilding and engineering for the rest of the trip! Or the change may have arisen from a variety of causes. The speed of the ship was not conducive to travel-comfort. There was an excessive vibration, and when the sea was rough the huge ship showed her ability to rise (and roll!) to the occasion, just too much for my liking. Indeed, one of the first things I did after my arrival in Toronto was to transfer my return booking to the Anchor-Donaldson liner, the *Athenia*. A very much smaller and slower ship than the *Leviathan* she took almost double the time to voyage, for the route this time was from Montreal to Glasgow via Liverpool. But every day was a sheer delight; the leisurely sail down the St. Lawrence; the sample of French colonisation afforded by the call at Quebec; the distant shores of the widening Gulf of St. Lawrence – those areas to which so many Highland families were driven under the pressure of eviction; the Newfoundland coast; the Straits of Belle Isle; and then the open seas until we glimpsed the welcoming lights of home.

I have good reason to cherish my memories of those months spent among our Scottish emigrants and Scots-Canadians to whom I ministered in 1927. From the moment of my arrival among them I was surrounded with kindness and understanding.

Alexander MacKenzie, a Gaelic-speaking Presbyterian elder hailing from Kirkhill, Inverness-shire, had already begun services for the emigrants in a small way, and his work was much appreciated. But now that the Church was considering extending the work there he was anxious to hand it over to someone who could give it more attention. Yet his heart was so much in it that complete withdrawal from it was out of the question. My debt to Mr. MacKenzie was incalculable. A more self-effacing helper would be hard to find, and the Free Church congregation that took form in Toronto regarded him with warm affection.

Central in my most cherished memories of those months in Toronto is Mrs. MacDonald, with whom I lodged. Bereft of her husband in her declining years, her native island of Bernera, Lewis, had no more to offer her. Her son and daughter had gone to Canada and had secured congenial occupation there; and a return to Bernera was out of the question. It was equally unthinkable to her son and

1. A view of the Sutherland hills near Elphin.

2. Dr. Collins' grandmother, Mrs. Dolina MacLeod, outside the croft house in Elphin.

3.   *Mr. Duncan MacRae, elder of the Free Church,*
     Elphin.

Free Gaelic Church, Greenock (Interior.)

4.   *Interior of the Gaelic Free Church, Greenock.*

                5.   *As Moderator of General Assembly in 194*

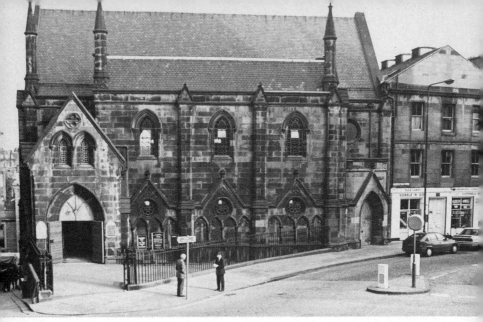

6. *Free St. Columba's Church where Dr. Collins was minister 1938–63.*

7. *The interior of St. Columba's, showing the canopied pulpit.*

8.   *The Moderamen at the Reformed Ecumenical Synod, Grand Rapids 1963: Dr. Collins*
     Professor John Murray, Professor Fred Klooster, Dr. Paul Schrotenboer, Professor
     Herman Ridderbos.

9. With his wife, Louisa, at the m[...]
   door of St. Columba's Churc[...]

10. The Free Church College,
    The Mound, Edinburgh.

11. Dr. Collins, as Convener of the Business Committee, bids farewell to the Queen after her visit to the Free Church Assembly in 1977.

daughter that she should be left there in lonely widowhood. So the counsel of common-sense prevailed, and she joined them in the land of their adoption.

If ever a woman embodied kindness and affection it was Mrs. MacDonald, and in Toronto she found what I feel was her true vocation. She was a Mary and Martha in one person. Her house became a true "home from home" for scores of young exiles, and her sincere Christian witness among them became to many a real means of grace. If I had judged my Gaelic inadequate to the strain of constant Gaelic preaching, my stay with Mrs. MacDonald was the providential remedy, for she spoke English only when she had to! The result for me was that my difficulty to *think* in Gaelic was soon remedied; for Mrs. MacDonald and I conversed together in Gaelic all the time. Toronto prepared me for the big event of the following year; my induction to the Free Gaelic Church in Greenock.

One morning, Mrs. MacDonald came to my room with a request. A young Lewisman had been on the phone with her to say that he and some of his friends would like to come to her house for family worship that evening. Would that be all right? And would she check with me?

There was no shadow of doubt as to the answer. They came; and that little meeting became like the rolling snowball which grows as it goes. Night by night they came, and my quite commodious sitting-room was filled by those young Highland expatriates who kept coming to join us in worship.

With some, it was a case of not missing the water until the well went dry. They were used to family worship in their old homes, and some of them confessed that there had been times when they had wished it had not been such a recognised part of family life. But now they were beginning to see things differently, and when the time for "the Book" came round, a feeling of emptiness and loss crept into their hearts. Actually, what was happening was that the Word, until now dormant in the heart, was beginning to assert itself and confront these young people with the greater issues of human life. In after years several of them made a public profession of their faith in Christ and were fruitful in His service.

The congregation fluctuated in numbers, for Toronto became very much a catchment area for emigrant Highlanders. From there, many of them moved west-wards, some indeed crossing the Border into the United States, and eventually making their homes there. But despite these depletions and other problems, the congregation founded in Toronto so many years ago continues as an outpost of the Free Church of Scotland; today, however, without the Gaelic services which meant so much to the original founders.

Probably the best-known names in evangelical ministerial circles there were those of Dr. A.B. Winchester, Dr. John Inkster and Dr. T.T. Shields. By that time, Dr. Winchester was Principal of the Bible College in Toronto, and Dr. Inkster had succeeded him in the pastorate of Knox Presbyterian Church. Dr. Shields was at the height of his tempestuous ministry in Jarvis Street Baptist Church. Somebody once said that his name ought to be *Swords*, not *Shields*, because of his constant forays against the theological Liberals, of whom the Canadian theological Colleges had not a few at the time – especially MacMaster University, now of Hamilton. But Shields was a magnificent preacher of the Gospel of grace, and a man of quite outstanding ability. In the warm weather he used to have an open-air meeting after his evening service; and, quite often, after our own service I crossed the park to sit under the arc-lights in the auditorium at the back of his church to hear a message from this "Canadian Spurgeon", as he was known.

Many years afterwards he preached for me in St. Columba's, Edinburgh. Before going into the pulpit, a portrait of Dr. Thomas Guthrie, which hangs in the vestry, caught his eye.

"What connection had Guthrie with this Church?" he asked. And when I told him that Guthrie was its first minister, as Free St. John's, he was thrilled. His father, he told me, was a great admirer of Guthrie, and had urged him to familiarise himself with Guthrie's published sermons and take him as his model. He was so glad to stand in Dr. Guthrie's pulpit that he went back to the Church the following day, accompanied by a photographer, so that he might have a picture of himself standing there. Shortly afterwards, it appeared in his magazine *The Gospel Witness*.

T.T. Shields was undoubtedly, as Dr. D. Martyn Lloyd-Jones describes him, "a truly great preacher, who was known throughout the Christian world", but also a man whose zeal was not always tempered with prudence. But when MacMaster capitulated to the Liberals, it was mainly due to the vision and courage of Shields that Toronto Baptist Seminary was founded as a College devoted to the Evangelical Faith.

My next visit to Canada was in 1930, by which time the Toronto congregation had grown considerably. It was still vacant, but was receiving almost continuous ministerial and student supply from Scotland, with the sustained and many-sided help of one of their own office-bearers, Mr. Malcolm Morrison, who later studied for the ministry and became the esteemed minister successively of Coigach, Scalpay, and Partick Highland. Rev. John MacSween M.A. was inducted as the first minister of Toronto Free Church in 1951, after giving it several earlier periods of service.

On this second visit to Canada my wife, Louisa, accompanied me. We travelled by the Anchor-Donaldson ship *Athenia*, docking in Montreal on Sabbath afternoon. The notice-board on a Church almost opposite our hotel informed us that Dr. Charles Gordon (better known as Ralph Connor, the novelist) would be preaching there that evening; so we decided to hear him. He preached on "The Impotence of the Church", based upon Mark 9:28, *Why could not we cast him out*? It was rather a rambling sermon, with some good flashes of thought here and there, but altogether showing more of the genius of the novelist than of the spiritual insight of the theologian.

Most of our time on this visit was spent in Fort William (now Thunderbay), Ontario. The congregation there was of longer standing, but had just recently become vacant by the return of their minister, Rev. Malcolm Galbraith, to Scotland.

Fort William was a relatively small town at that time, and had a very efficient intelligence service due to the fact that almost everyone was on the phone, and the rental of the instrument covered the cost of all local calls. News was sometimes in short supply, but one of the carriers who met the few trains that called there each day could always be depended upon to come up with something! His special line on the night that we arrived was that the train had deposited "twenty firkins of salt herring from Scotland, and a Gaelic minister" — in that order of uncertain priority! Not much to get excited about, you might think, but the carrier knew that there were many people in Fort William and Port Arthur who had a strong addiction both to salt herring and Gaelic ministers!

The winter was bitterly cold, even for that region, but my wife and I enjoyed our brisk walks in the sunshine when it was not snowing. Wheeled traffic was sometimes difficult, and horse-drawn sleighs were common. The very perambulators were on runners, and several of the people used skis and snow-shoes. The Red Indian settlement at Chippewa was an unfailing source of interest, and we used to wonder at the muted exuberances of the Indian children at their games until we were told that they were trained to quietness lest they should scare away the game and wild animals which the men-folk hunted and from which they drew much of their livelihood.

Sometimes we walked out on to the solid ice of Lake Superior, and watched the men lowering their fishing tackle through the large, circular holes they had cut through the ice to get at the fish.

The huge grain elevators by the Lake, and the massive grain-ships, for the present locked in by the ice, indicated the importance of the grain trade to the community. Many of our people were connected with it, and some of them rose to high positions in its management.

Quite a large contingent of the Gaelic-speaking Highlanders had settled in the Fort William area around 1910, and in 1913 they built for themselves a frame building, with a considerable congregation there by the time of the later emigrations. Among these older emigrants there was no more influential man than Murdo MacKay. When Murdo emigrated to Canada he took his home religion with him and did his utmost to transplant it in Canadian soil. Some opposed him in this and regarded him as altogether too rigid. Yet he retained his place among them, and there could have been few more highly-esteemed men in the town than Murdo MacKay.

Murdo once stayed with us in Edinburgh, and I had the pleasure of taking him around many of the places associated with the Reformation and the Covenanting movements. The last place of this kind to which I took him was the Protestant Institute Hall, where one of my elders, James MacDonald, was curator at the time. At my request, James produced one of our most prized Covenanter relics – the sword of the gallant and godly Captain John Paton, who was put to death in 1684 in the Grassmarket of Edinburgh for his part in Scotland's struggle for Spiritual Independence.

"Take the sword in your hand," I urged him. He gripped it by the hilt and as he raised it to an upright position to see it better, he, as John Bunyan would say, "looked, and looked again, even till the springs that were in his head sent the waters down his cheeks."

And that is how I like to remember him – a man of Reformed principles who, had he lived in the days of the Covenant, would have been out with the "men of the moss-hags" even to the danger of his very life. That was the kind of man he was; stubbornly uncompromising, perhaps, but true as steel,

One who never turned his back, but marched breast-forward
Never doubted clouds would break
Never dreamed, though right were worsted, wrong would triumph
Held we fall to rise, are baffled to fight better,
Sleep to wake.

We returned home on this occasion via New York, for I had some engagements to fulfil on the American side along the route. From New York we sailed by the Anchor line *Cameronia*. It was on a Saturday afternoon, and we were not long aboard when a junior officer came to our cabin with a message; "Captain's compliments, Sir. And would you kindly take Divine Service for us tomorrow?"

I agreed, but soon began to regret my rashness; for we were scarcely clear of the Hudson when a storm blew up. The items of luggage "wanted on the voyage" which we had stowed away under the lower berth of our cabin simply defied all our attempts to anchor them, and kept banging from wall to wall all the night through. Comparatively few turned up for breakfast next morning, and the prospects for "Divine Service" afterwards were anything but bright. When the congregation did eventually assemble, the unspoken plea for brevity was irresistible, and even then, we had some slight casualties. When we tried, later, to settle in the main lounge we were still at risk. At one point a massive piano broke loose from its moorings at the wall and went careering across the room. We crowded into broad-cased arm-chairs and couches, and several of the younger set, with good sense, simply sat, or lay, on the carpets. The *Cameronia* provided all manner of unrehearsed diversion for our entertainment, but few appreciated her ingenuity. Now and again the storm abated somewhat, but always blew up again. Not, indeed, until after we got into the lee of the Irish coast did we reach calm seas again. And although by then we had regained our sea-legs, it was a pleasant experience to plant our feet on *terra firma* once more.

12: The Free Gaelic Church, Greenock

The congregation to which I was inducted in June 1928 had an interesting history. It had its roots in the old Gaelic Chapel of Greenock which, at the time of the Disruption in 1843, had Rev. Angus MacBean as its minister. When the split came in May of that year, almost the whole congregation followed him into the Free Church.

Deprived of their Church buildings, they worshipped for a time in a large marquee, erected in the Duncan Street burying-ground. But by September 1844 their new Church in Jamaica Street was ready for occupation. It was a plain, commodious building, originally seating 1500 people, and with a congregation to match. My senior elder when I went to Greenock, Captain Donald Shaw, once told me that when his parents came with their family from Jura to make their home in Gourock, and connected themselves with the Free Gaelic Church, they had to wait three years before they could have their own pew; for those were the days of the family pew. This calculation signifies that in the 1870's the Free Gaelic was still a very full Church.

Angus MacBean's ministry in Greenock ended in 1845, and he was succeeded by Rev. John MacRae, popularly known in Gaelic circles as "*MacRath Mor*" (Big MacRae). MacRae was a mighty preacher, and his word was with power. He had seen and experienced so much of the evils of strong drink that he lost no opportunity of speaking out against it. One day, in the Free Gaelic, he did so with such effect that a publican present sought out a fellow-tradesman in the congregation and proposed that they should meet for a chat the following day. They agreed and comparisons revealed that they were both troubled about the same matter. They were both in the drink-trade and, by worldly standards, "doing well". But MacRae's sermon had convinced them both that they must get out. So they went into partnership in setting up a wholesale grocery business that made the firm of MacFarlan and Shearer familiar throughout the country.

One day, while visiting in the Gabriel Wood Mariners' Home in

Greenock, I was hailed by a very old man, a retired sailor, who was sitting by the fire.

"Are you the new minister of the Free Gaelic Church?" he enquired.

And when I replied that I was, he continued, "And did you ever hear of 'Big MacRae'?" "Yes" I nodded.

"Well." he proceeded, "it was he who baptised me, in the Free Gaelic Church."

It was my only living link with Big MacRae's ministry in Greenock.

Mr. MacRae was succeeded there by John Kennedy — a cousin of the more famous Dr. John Kennedy of Dingwall. Mr. Kennedy was a man of rather delicate health, and he died in Greenock after a ministry of around 11 years.

Rev. Murdoch MacAskill came next in succession, and during his time the Church building underwent considerable interior alterations which reduced its seating accommodation, but increased its comfort. Mr. MacAskill was a preacher of note and, for a time, was prominent among the Constitutionalist Party in the denomination, who were resisting certain doctrinal adaptations that were under discussion with a view to union with the United Presbyterian Church. But, at almost the last moment, he changed sides. Good Archie Crawford, of Kames, saw it coming, and expostulated with him. Comparing Mr. MacAskill to a trick-rider in a circus, he said, "You, Mr. MacAskill, are trying to ride two horses with a foot on each horse, and you won't succeed. The end of you will be that you will fall between them."

The forecast came sadly true. By then Mr. MacAskill had left Greenock to succeed Dr. Kennedy in Dingwall — a move that had made him a prime target for the Unionist Party in the Church. Outmanoeuvred by their supreme strategist, Principal Rainy, Mr. MacAskill, in 1897, changed sides and became a bitter opponent of the Constitutionalists who were still holding out, and in 1900 entered the United Free Church. Three years later his race was run. In his last illness he sent for his former fellow-campaigner and co-presbyter, Rev. Finlay MacRae of Plockton, but what passed between these two good men neither of them ever disclosed. But Murdoch MacAskill had the solace of knowing that his former brethren who had continued in the ministry of the Free Church had not cast him off. And it was at his own request that one of them, Rev. Murdo Mackenzie, of the Free North Church, Inverness, took the Gaelic memorial service in Dingwall on the Sabbath after his death.

The Greenock Free Gaelic Church had been unsettled by Mr. MacAskill's ecclesiastical brinkmanship, and a small number had seceded to form a congregation of the Free Presbyterian Church at the time of the Declaratory Act controversy. Under the ministry of Rev. John Campbell, who succeeded Mr. MacAskill, the congregation declined considerably, and in 1900 a majority of them had gone over to the United Free Church, still claiming the right to remain in possession of both Church and Manse. The Parliamentary Executive Commission of 1905, however, awarded both buildings to the remaining Free Church congregation, and they took up their work again in their old home. They called Rev. Roderick Macleod B.D. from Canada in 1908, but his stay with them was not long, for in 1910 he accepted a call from the large congregation of Knock, Lewis. He was succeeded in Greenock by Rev. Kenneth Smith who, after a short ministry, joined the Church of Scotland.

It was thus to a congregation greatly weakened by desertions, short ministries and long vacancies that Rev. William Macleod M.A. of Shiskine succeeded in 1923. Under his capable ministry the congregation rallied promisingly; but Clydeside did not suit his health, and in January 1928 he accepted a call to Dornoch. This time the vacancy was not long. Just five months after his departure I was ordained and inducted to the charge.

Greenock's attraction for me was certainly not that of material prosperity or physical comfort. What drew me to it I cannot even yet say. I was always a lover of the country, and my natural bent was to a congregation in rural surroundings, and there were still plenty of these on offer. Five of them actually approached me with a view to proceeding with a call, but let me hastily add that such situations were not uncommon in those years. The Rev. John Noble of Lairg was interim-moderator for a vacancy in his own Presbytery and there was an understanding between him and a certain final year student who had signified his deep interest in the congregation, as they had in him, that, as soon as he was licensed, he would confirm to Mr. Noble that — other things being equal — he was now ready to consider a call from the congregation in question. But when the time came the young licentiate told the interim-moderator that the situation had changed; two other congregations had approached him since last they had discussed the vacancy in which he had been so interested. And he was hearing that there might be another!

But Mr. Noble would have none of it. "Tut, Sir, tut," he ejaculated, "don't let that mislead you. When I was a probationer there were about 16 probationers for every vacancy to choose from, but today there are about 16 vacancies for every probationer. It's not a compliment, Sir; it's sheer necessity; sheer necessity."

The situation had eased in the intervening years, but even in 1928 there was little risk of becoming a "stickit minister!" But it was Greenock, the least attractive of the vacancies that had approached me, that actually gripped. So, on the 20th of June, 1928, and by appointment of the Free Church Presbytery of Glasgow, the Rev. D.G. Ferguson of Ayr presiding, I was ordained to the ministry of the Word, and inducted to the Free Gaelic Church, after a most appropriate sermon on the words in 1 Timothy 3:15, *"...the church of the living God, the pillar and ground of the truth."* And the Sabbath following, my good friend, Rev. John Macleod O.B.E., whose assistant I had been in Hope Street Free Church, Glasgow, introduced me with a thoughtful sermon on Micah 6:8, *"He hath shewed thee, O man, what is good; and what doth the Lord require of thee, but to do justly, and to love mercy, and to walk humbly with thy God?"*

My own first text as minister of the congregation I took as primarily a word from the Lord to myself as I took up His yoke, *"My grace is sufficient for thee; for My strength is made perfect in weakness"* (2 Cor. 12:9). As I was leaving the church that night a lady – whom I came to know afterwards as one of the godliest persons in the congregation – slipped a folded paper into my hand as I bade her good-night. I read it after I got home, and this is what she had written:

WELCOME! *"The Lord recompense thy work, and a full reward be given thee of the Lord God of Israel, under whose wings thou art come to trust" (Ruth 2:12).*

Silently, I prayed God that the word to the stranger from Moab in her new surroundings might be a word to me in mine.

Economically, Greenock was not a prosperous town in the early years of my ministry, and the situation worsened with the passing years. There was a slump in the heavy industries on which the town depended. The Clydeside "hungry thirties"were on their way. As the depression deepened we could see across the river, as we travelled to and from Glasgow, the rusting hull of the mammoth Cunarder, the *Queen Mary*, lying silent on the stocks in John Brown's famous yard at Clydebank for lack of money to complete her. The times were hard and daily getting harder, but they had their compensations. There are indeed lessons that we learn in the shadows that we could never learn in the sunshine.

To minister to a people involved in unemployment and its

attendant miseries meant, as it did to Ezekiel when he served his captive brethren in Babylon, that one had "to sit where they sat." Only thus could one cultivate a helpful sympathy with them and see the hand of God in their trials. There were some, of course, who resorted to the vain consolation of cynical complaint against Divine Providence. But there were others who turned anxiety to prayer, and learned to sing "songs in the night". I can never doubt that we came through that testing time more closely knit together in fellowship, more enriched in spirit, more understanding in judgment than we had been before our faith was tried. It was an excellent, though testing, training for a young minister.

In the year following my induction, the union between the Church of Scotland and the United Free Church of Scotland took place, as a result of which some who had belonged to the Free Church of Scotland prior to 1900 returned to their former loyalty and were a great help to the congregation.

In recreational and social amenity Greenock had much to offer. There was no nationalisation of Railway and Steamship services in those days, and this was not to the loss of the travelling public. The rivalry between the competing companies meant better transport facilities and more adequate services, not to speak of keener fares.

The afternoon and evening cruises in the summer months were specially popular. For prices ranging from one shilling to one shilling and sixpence one could obtain cruise tickets to Kilcreggan, Gareloch, the Holy Loch and Dunoon; and for a few additional pence cruises were available round Bute, round Arran and to places down the coast. Four hours sailing, in some cases, for as little as two shillings or half a crown! Bus services were beginning to catch up as rival pleasure transport, and there were excursion fares to Glasgow on certain days for as little as two shillings, and one and eightpence! But who wanted to go to Glasgow in the summer-time?

Best of all, when the weather was good, were the walks round the Cut, or up the Gryfe, or across the hills to Inverkip. We soon learned that it was prudent to have a light rain-coat handy, but even on occasions of imprudence, when we got soaked through, it did not dampen our ardour, and we always maintained that Greenock rain was the kindliest variety that fell anywhere.

It took the threat of war to bring revival to the heavy industries of Clydeside, but it was soon realised that this was merely a temporary boost, and that the pride of achievement implied in the slogan "Clyde-built" was fast becoming a fading echo of better days.

My name was still on Admiralty Fleet Orders as an Officiating-Chaplain to Presbyterian, and certain other, naval personnel when Greenock came into prominence as a naval base in the Second World War, although, by that time, I had removed to Edinburgh. The office had been almost a complete sinecure in peace time, but when, after the Scapa Flow disaster, large numbers of our armed merchant cruisers gathered into the safer waters of the Clyde estuary, Greenock almost overnight came into naval prominence and the chaplaincy grew in importance correspondingly. For some time, until it could be transferred to my successor in the Free Gaelic Church — the Rev. John Murdo Macleod — I had, with his collaboration, to plan and organise the work among Presbyterian personnel. With characteristic enthusiasm, Mr. Macleod threw himself into the new duty assigned him; and with the backing of the Free Church Chaplaincy Committee, and a generous financial grant from *An Comunn Gaidhealach*, we opened a new rest and recreation centre in the hall of the Reformed Presbyterian Church which was closely adjacent to our own. The *"Aros"*, as we called it, was a popular centre with the service-men, and the Church parades in the Free Gaelic Church were well attended. The Church building itself received a battle-scar in one of the air raids on the town but was repaired and kept in service. But the human fabric was more difficult to restore.

The difficulty in this direction was simple, but not open to remedy. The congregation had a considerable constituency of domestic servants, most of them from the Western Isles, who, after the 1939-45 War broke out, were almost completely mopped up by being drafted into National Service of one kind or another, or by being recalled home to take the places of the men-folk there who had been called up for the Royal Navy, or other branches of the armed services. By the time the War was over, society had been levelled out to such an extent that stately homes with a staff of servants had virtually become things of the past. This, with the stagnation of the basic industries, brought about a slump from which Greenock has never fully recovered.

The Free Gaelic Church, in common with other predominantly working-class congregations, was severely reduced in numbers. It had long and competent ministries afterwards, but never regained its former strength.

The commodious old building, with its excellent acoustics, became too costly to maintain. The larger of its halls became adequate for the needs of the diminished flock. But a loyal and whole-hearted remnant continues to maintain its evangelical witness, and the potential for growth is still there, but no longer on the Gaelic side of the work. Of the once famous Gaelic Chapel which largely emptied itself into the Free Church of Scotland in 1843 nothing remains. The section of the Free Gaelic congregation which, in turn, went into the United Free Church in 1900 has also disappeared, and their Church is closed. The prospect of revival for the Gaelic language on the Clydeside ecclesiastical scene is dim indeed; but for all who long for spiritual revival the promise of God stands firm, and all who plead it can do so with the same confidence as was expressed by John Wesley in testing times,

"The best of all is, God is with us."

13: Free St. Columba's, Edinburgh

I began my tenth year in Greenock without any thought that it might be my last. I was happy in my pastorate. The lines, I felt, had fallen to me in pleasant places. No minister could have had a more loyal band of office-bearers to work with, or a more pleasant set of people to serve in the Gospel. Over the years there had been one or two attempts to call me to other spheres of labour, but in no case did I feel a sense of call, and I acted accordingly.

The next approach of this kind was totally unexpected.

Dr. Alexander Stewart of St. Columba's had died quite suddenly in April 1937, and when, in due time, a move was made towards a new pastoral settlement, my name was submitted and accepted. There had been no attempt, official or otherwise, to ascertain my mind in the matter, and my first intimation of what had happened came through a paragraph in the *Greenock Telegraph* to the effect that I had been elected to the charge of Free St. Columba's, Edinburgh. My immediate impulse was to stop all proceedings, but I could not very well do so on the strength of a press report. At the same time I had a growing fear that my office-bearers might think it strange that I had not confided in them in the matter. I therefore wrote to Rev. R. M. Knox, who was the interim-moderator of the vacancy, explaining my predicament, and requesting him, if indeed the report of the St. Columba election was true, to be so kind as to stop all proceedings, for I had no desire, nor sense of duty, to leave my present charge for another.

Mr. Knox wrote a kindly and understanding reply, confirming the accuracy of the report, but requesting me not to withdraw at this stage. If, nearer the time fixed for the signing of the call, I was still of that mind, nobody could fault me for having let matters go so far, inasmuch as they had not consulted me in the first instance.

Reluctantly, I complied, but still with the intention of stopping the call if and when it reached my own Presbytery, unless, in the interval, some clear indication was given me that it was my duty to accept the call. And the "clear indication" that I had principally in mind was that an inclination towards St. Columba's might be given me that would be strong enough to overcome my extreme reluctance to leave Greenock. But while I waited, my bond with the Free Gaelic

Church seemed to grow stronger with each passing day. That, I concluded, was decisive. God's guidance was that I should remain where I was. So, one night, late though it was, I wrote a letter to Mr. Knox telling him that events had confirmed my belief that my duty was to remain in my present charge.

By this time it was around midnight. The pillar-box was just across the street from the Manse, but I decided not to post my letter until the following morning, lest the sound of unlocking and locking doors should disturb the members of the household who had already retired.

My slumber that night was sweet! The matter was now finished!

Next morning, however, in going through my mail, I came across a letter from a correspondent with whose script I was sufficiently familiar to know his identity before opening his letter. It was from Rev. Peter Chisholm of Lochalsh, a man with whom I seldom corresponded. It was a brief message and to my great surprise, related to the call from St. Columba's. It simply said this:

"You are much in my thoughts these days because of the call addressed to you by St. Columba's. That is a matter into which I must not enter in any detail. But I feel constrained to write to you only to say this; *personal inclinations, however strong they may be, are not necessarily infallible indications of Divine guidance.*"

I was astounded. This could not be mere accident. That one sentence threw me back into indecision. My letter was never posted, and when the St. Columba call was eventually placed in my hands by the Presbytery I accepted it, still disinclined to change to another field of service, but now convinced that it was my duty to do so.

Some years later, while staying with my former fellow-student, Donald A. MacRae in his manse at Lochranza, Donald recalled an incident of student days. On our way home from a prayer-meeting in St. Columba's, where Dr. Stewart had given an excellent Bible-Reading from the Book of Proverbs, I had remarked, "Donald, do you know two things I should not want to happen to me?"

Of course he did not, but he wanted to know what they were.

"Well," I said, "I should not like to make my home in Edinburgh; and even more, I should not like to be the man who will succeed Dr. Stewart in St. Columba's."

"And now that both things have happened," said my friend, "are you still of the same mind?"

The reply was an emphatic negative!

I was inducted to my new charge on January 19th 1938, by Professor Alexander Ross D.D., of the Free Church College, and formally introduced to the congregation the following Sabbath morning by my predecessor's life- long friend, Rev. George Mackay of Fearn who, towards the end of his sermon, said something that comforted me not a little. "And now," he said, "I am going to tell you something that I decided to keep to myself until after you had chosen your new minister." He referred to a chat that Dr. John Macleod and he had had with Dr. Stewart in the St. Columba's manse some months before Dr. Stewart's last illness. The conversation was partly in bantering strain. Somehow the subject of longevity had cropped up, and Principal Macleod had remarked that Dr. Stewart himself was of long-lived stock. "Very likely then," said Mr. Mackay to Dr. Stewart, "John and I will be away before you, so, if you are still Editor of the *Monthly Record*, see that you provide us with good obituaries!"

But Dr. Stewart was not in a mood to be teased, and expressed his belief that both his friends would outlive him.

"Where then" said Mr. Mackay, "shall we find your successor?"

"That duty," replied Dr. Stewart, "will fall to others, "but for myself," he added, "I would regard as, all in all, the most suitable man for the charge, George Collins of Greenock."

Mr. Mackay went on to say that he now told the congregation of this conversation because he felt that it would please them to know that the minister of their choice would also have been the choice of their former pastor for them if he had any say in the matter.

What effect, if any, this disclosure had upon the congregation I never knew, but personally, it touched me deeply (a) because I valued the judgment of my former pastor, although I profoundly disagreed with it in this particular instance; (b) because Mr. Mackay and Dr. Macleod had had the good sense to say nothing about this incident until the congregation had made their independent choice, and I had made mine; and (c) because it helped to confirm the sense of Divine guidance that had eventually prevailed upon me to accept the St. Columba's call. No minister ever had less reason to regret his choice than I had in my long ministry in St. Columba's.

I had made many friends in the congregation in student days, and they welcomed me back and gave me the heartiest support in the work. Three ladies in particular call for mention. They were sisters, Agnes, Jane and Margaret Niven. They had no aspiration to ordained office in the Church and were well content with the places assigned to women in the New Testament Church. They were tireless workers in the Sabbath School, the Women's Bible Class, and the

Women's Mission. Nobody knew the congregation better than they did, and they were constantly on the move – doing good by stealth. Miss Jane had a special flair for visitation. Often and often on a Monday morning my phone would ring and Miss Jane would be there to tell me of someone whom she had missed from Church the day before, and on whom she had called that morning to see if all was well. If not, she would tell me, so that I might take the appropriate action. But if the person concerned just happened to have a slight cold that morning, or to be away from home for the weekend, she would still phone to tell me "to save me an unnecessary call."

How many hours of service and miles of travel Miss Jane spared me — especially in my early years in St. Columba's — it would be difficult to compute.

My first year in Edinburgh was in the uneasy period before the Second World War – the war that so many were convinced, even to the last moment, would never happen. The noisy Nazis that corporal Hitler had gathered around him were not to be taken too seriously. Their posing and prancing and sabre-rattling might indeed cause alarm in the Eastern States of Europe, but they would never face up to the might of the West! Or if they did, it would be to their own quick annihilation! Jingoism was strong in those days.

I was in London over the weekend following the *Anschluss* of March 1938, and, by the kindness of Sir Murdoch MacDonald – then M.P. for Inverness-shire – was able to hear the debate in the House of Commons after the event. The speaking was spirited, but even yet the gravity of the developing situation in Europe did not appear to cause alarm, and the conversations in the dining-room of the House were lightly optimistic.

Hitler's war-machine had shown but little of its boasted efficiency in the *Anschluss*, and there had been several embarrassing breakdowns in his military equipment. He would not dare to attempt anything really big with such inadequate armaments! There was certainly no need for panic!

A rousing speech by Winston Churchill crowded the House, but, quite clearly, did not appear to alert the Commons as it was meant to do. Neville Chamberlain seemed most complacent of all and still appeared to regard his critics as alarmists who were doing an ill-service to the nation by their calls to action. The war of words in the debating chamber settled down again to an uncertain truce.

When, on Sabbath, 3rd September 1939, the drone of Goering's *Luftwaffe* brought the air-raid sirens into operation over

Edinburgh, the people's reaction was understandably one of consternation. In my absence from home that day, my pulpit was occupied by Principal Macleod, who had just returned from the United States on the *Athenia*. It was, incidentally, her last crossing of the Atlantic, for on her return journey she was sunk by a German U-boat.

When on that Sabbath Edinburgh had its first air-raid warning the congregations, for the most part, were in Church at the forenoon service, and several of the preachers quietly dismissed their congregations and advised them to make their way to the nearest air-raid shelters. Not so my substitute in St. Columba's. He calmly continued the service as if nothing had happened, thereby communicating his own strength to his hearers. The alert was soon cancelled, and all the arrangements for the day were carried through as if nothing had happened. That was the kind of man Principal Macleod was.

That alert, however, was a needed reminder that we were now a country at war, and that the programme of the Church would have to be drastically adapted to meet the changed situation. With the winter drawing near, there could be no more evening services until "black-out" regulations had been fully met. Sunday Schools, normally conducted outside Church service times, had to meet concurrently with the forenoon service so as to ensure that children would not be left unaccompanied in the darkened streets. As time went on, several of them were evacuated to the country for safety.

There was no saying when the *Luftwaffe* might decide to look us up. Driving down Leith Walk on the afternoon of October 16th 1939, I noticed some unfamiliar air-craft flying rather low over the Firth of Forth while puffs as of anti-aircraft shells kept exploding around them. I decided to get out of that area as quickly as I could, but with no more serious thought than that the R.A.F. were having a practice, for I had not heard the alert. Later on, as I was making my way to our mid-week prayer-meeting, I became aware of an excited little group in the Lawnmarket who had been watching a convoy of service vehicles driving up to Edinburgh Castle. It was a common enough sight, but, for some reason, this particular convoy had aroused special interest.

"What's happening?" I asked one of our elders who was standing by.

"Oh", he said, "it's the sequel to the air-raid. The survivors from the German planes which were shot down over the Forth were taken captive, and have just been taken into the Castle."

So it had been the real thing after all! Hitler's first raid on the Forth had been a complete failure, and some of his men were beginning what was to be a long experience of Scotland's war-time hospitality.

Edinburgh suffered comparatively little from the *Luftwaffe*. We had frequent alerts, but the real objectives of the raiders were the shipbuilding yards and heavy industries of Glasgow and the lower Clyde. We could hear the quite distinctive sound of their engines as they passed over us, and their bombing, for the most part, seemed incidental and random — perhaps just a jettisoning of what remained of their deadly cargo as they limped back on their way home.

Only once during the long years of war did we, as a congregation, suffer any special inconvenience from the air-raids. A Gaelic Fellowship meeting had just begun on the Friday evening of our Communion season when our peace was shattered by the raucous alert of the air-raid sirens, and almost simultaneously by the thunder of the nearby Castle batteries. Questioning glances were exchanged. There were air-raid shelters in the vicinity, but could they give us any better protection than the stout walls which encircled us where we were? Besides, the falling flak had to be reckoned with if we went out into the streets. What went up must come down.

In the circumstances, I suggested that we stay where we were and continue our meeting, but left it entirely to the judgment of everyone present whether to go or stay.

Not a person moved; and soon our attention was recaptured for the purpose of our gathering. The last speaker was on his feet when the sirens shrilled their "all clear". And the text for the evening had been *"Blessed is the people that know the joyful sound!"* (Psalm 89:15).

There seemed to be only one Psalm with which to close the meeting that night; and we sang it;

> *God is our refuge and our strength,*
> *in straits a present aid;*
> *Therefore, although the earth remove,*
> *we will not be afraid.*   (Psalm 46:1).

That night, I believe, we sang it with greater conviction than ever before. In after years I used to meet, from time to time, people who had been present at that meeting who spoke of it as one of the most edifying meetings of its kind that they had ever attended. One of them, a worthy elder of the Church, used to say, "I felt wrapped round with Psalm 91." I knew what he meant, for I recalled having had the same feeling.

> *His feathers shall thee hide; thy trust*
> *under His wings shall be;*
> *His faithfulness shall be a shield*
> *and buckler unto thee.* (Psalm 91:4).

But when Adolf Hitler perished ingloriously by his own hand on 30th April 1945, he bequeathed to Edinburgh, and to every region upon which the foul shadow of Nazism had fallen, a legacy of trouble that has not, even yet, been expended, and a new order which is not a change for the better.

We were celebrating the centenary of St. Columba's as the war in Europe was drawing to its close, and our special preacher for the occasion was Dr. D. M. Lloyd-Jones of Westminster Chapel, London. He had finished his engagements with us, but had to cancel one in Newcastle, which he was to have taken on his way back, because he had announced to his congregation that if the end of the war came suddenly, as seemed likely, they were to assume that there would be a thanksgiving service in the Chapel the following evening.

I was in London the following Lord's Day taking the Gaelic V.E. Day Thanksgiving Service in Crown Court Church in the afternoon, and I attended Westminster Chapel in the evening.

When I joined Dr. Lloyd-Jones in his vestry afterwards and asked what his text had been at his Thanksgiving service, he replied, "Hitler's text, of course."

"Which was...?"

He quoted Psalm 37:35,36:- *I have seen the wicked in great power, and spreading himself like a green bay tree. Yet he passed away, and, lo, he was not; I sought him, but he could not be found.*

The words were so truly descriptive of the rise and fall of the German Fuehrer that they might have been written on his epitaph.

Those years of the war-time ministry in the cities imposed a strain that God-given strength alone could meet. Our brethren in the West suffered more than we did in the East, but we never knew when our time might come. Visits to people bereft of their loved ones in the various fields of conflict were a constant heartache, and an unyielding strain on our physical and emotional strength. We were all in this together. We came to dread the bright moonlight lest it should bring the German planes. Almost equally we learned to fear the dark nights when we had to be out of doors, for the stringency of the "black-out" regulations, together with the natural darkness, made the very crossing of a street a major hazard.

Perhaps my most poignant memory of those times was a visit that I paid to Greenock on the day after one of their worst air-raids. I had been in Glasgow overnight, and felt that I could not go back to Edinburgh without news of my former congregation.

But how could I obtain contact with them? The railways were cut; the roads scarcely usable at points; and the telephone lines torn apart. The town was virtually *incommunicado*. Transport time-tables had become quite meaningless overnight.

In St. Enoch Square I happened to find a bus just leaving for Greenock, and managed to obtain standing-room on it, although it was already overcrowded. Normal safety regulations were relaxed in the existing emergency.

Greenock was a ghastly sight that morning. The devastation of the night before had left it well-nigh unrecognisable. When, at length, I reached my former Manse I found my successor, Rev. John M. Macleod, in a state of utter bewilderment after those hours of devilry. He had already opened his doors to a family in the congregation whose house had been made utterly uninhabitable, and he was just setting out to look for an old lady of frail health who lived alone. At his request I accompanied him. We found her in what must have been the only unharmed tenement in the block.

She was quite serene. "I could not go to the air-raid shelter," she explained, "so I just asked the Lord to shelter me where I was. And He did. So I'm staying on. Just before the raid," she explained, "I was reading the 54th chapter of Isaiah, and was specially impressed by the words in verse 17, '*No weapon that is formed against thee shall prosper...*' so I just took the Lord at His word." And from that moment, she was quite sure there was no weapon in Hitler's armoury that could pierce her defences.

The obituary notices in the *Greenock Telegraph* the next day showed how great the loss of life had been, but before the day was done we concluded that, despite a great deal of damage to the fabric of their homes, the congregation had not sustained a fatal casualty.

Quite early in the War I had taken over Dr. Donald Maclean's place as the Free Church representative on the Chaplaincy Board at the War Office, and this, along with some other recurring commitments, necessitated frequent journeys to London. One of these was a day or two after the centre of the old city of London was almost burned to a shell by a particularly heavy raid. I have told elsewhere of my thoughts as I walked through the devastated area.

Had we come to the end of our civilisation? Had the world gone quite mad?

It was a dull, damp morning and the leaden skies seemed to weep sullenly and despairingly over a lost cause. But suddenly, there was a slight break in the clouds, and a thin shaft of light, as of a sick sunbeam, shone for a moment on the great gilded cross which surmounts St. Paul's Cathedral, which I could just see above gaunt and broken walls.

Now, I have always been cautious of symbols which may too easily become objects of undue veneration, but I confess that for that moment the shining cross of St. Paul's flashed a message of hope into my drooping soul. And a voice, loud and clear as a clarion, seemed to sound from beyond those weeping skies, "... *the Lord will not cast off His people, neither will He forsake His inheritance; but judgment shall return unto righteousness; and all the upright in heart shall follow it.*" (Psalm 94:14,15).

14: From Pulpit to Rostrum

When, in 1962, Dr. A.M. Renwick intimated his intention to retire from the Chair of Church History in the Free Church College, nothing was farther from my mind than that I should be nominated as his successor. True, I had been proposed for the post when it became vacant by the death of Dr. Maclean, but I had no hesitation on that occasion in requesting that my name be withdrawn.

In the event Dr. Renwick was elected, and a better appointment could hardly have been made. Of Border stock, but of Highland birth and upbringing, he was a mixture of opposites, and a splendid blend it turned out to be. Loyal and courageous to the core, he would have made a splendid Border Covenanter had he lived in their time. But the Celtic strain predominated, and no clansman would have followed his chief, "Gu buaidh no gu bas" (To vict'ry or death), with more complete devotion than he. Patriot, idealist, enthusiast and mystic met in him, and the combination never seemed incongruous. The Constitutional party in the Free Church commanded his admiration from his youth, and when he decided to study for the ministry his denominational affinity was not for a moment in doubt, although he was in civil service employment in Manchester when the moment of decision came.

He was minister of the Dumbarton Free High Church when the Foreign Missions appealed to him to go to Lima to succeed Dr. John A. Mackay in the head-mastership of the Church's College there. He went from a sense of duty more than from personal choice, and the going involved a considerable element of domestic readjustment and self-sacrifice. So, in 1943, when the Church called him back, he came, and for 19 years gave distinguished service in the Free Church College.

On his retiral, my name came up again for the vacancy. I was not present when the nomination was made in my own Presbytery and when at the next meeting I proposed to withdraw, I was informed that, by that time, several other Presbyteries had put forward my name, so that my withdrawal in Edinburgh Presbytery would not prevent its inclusion in the list of returns which the Training of the Ministry Committee would lay before the General Assembly. Better let my nomination stand until then. And so I did; but in the event, and yielding to the advice of some senior ministers, I let it be put to the Assembly, with the consequence that my pastoral connection with St. Columba's was ended by my induction to the Church History chair in 1963. The change in ministry was not easily made, but there is no doubting the importance that the Church has in its best days attached to the maintenance of a well trained ministry — even, at times, to the translation of ministers against their inclination from the charges in which they were serving to the College chairs where, in the judgment of the General Assembly of the Church, they were more urgently needed.

I found, to my great relief, that there are compensatory features in academic service. For example, it became easier to respond to appeals for special help from brethren all over the Church. The carefully planned programme of the College enabled one to measure spare time and decide how much of this could be devoted to writing and research. Fellowship with scholars of evangelical Colleges in other lands was greatly facilitated also, and proved richly rewarding.

For some years after the Church Union in Scotland the dissenting party who continued the Free Church of Scotland had to endure ostracism and disparagement from brethren in the discredited majority to whose changed creed they refused to adapt.

Now the trend was changing. Theological students from other denominations were opting to take certain classes in the Free Church College in preference to those provided in the Universities, where the tendency was to move farther and farther away from the doctrines of grace as formulated by the Reformers. The Free Presbyterian Church of Eastern Australia sought and obtained mutual eligibility with the Free Church, and from the outset several of their students trained with us. Students came from Germany, Czechoslovakia, the Netherlands and America and shared our training, and in this way new bonds were formed between the Reformed Churches of Europe and the U.S.A. The signs of the times were brightening. Outmoded Liberalism was being rejected. Calvinism was on the upsurge. When in 1927, and as a result of the Davey heresy trial in the Irish Presbyterian Church, the Irish Evangelical Church came into existence, their students too, for the most part, came to the Free Church College for training, and a warm and mutually helpful association was formed between the two Churches.

I was, at the time, contributing a series of articles to the *Monthly Record* of the Free Church, which caught the attention of Rev.

W.J. Grier who was contemporaneously editing *The Irish Evangelical*, and led to a warm fellowship being formed between us. Mr. Grier wrote to Dr. Stewart requesting permission to reproduce some of these articles in his own magazine. Dr. Stewart passed the request on to me, and in this way introduced me to one of my closest friends. Jim Grier was a rare soul, scholarly, cultured, humble, gracious and unfailingly courteous, even in the midst of controversy. He had played a leading role in arraigning Professor Davey on a charge of heresy and was vilified by the Liberals in the case as a disturber of the peace, but it would take more ingenuity than his detractors could command to make their charge stick. Controversy was foreign to Jim's nature.

He had been brought up in Irish Evangelicalism in its finest quality, and in post-graduate study had gone to Princeton Theological Seminary. The result was to confirm him in the faith of his fathers, and to make him more zealous in its proclamation. He believed that, as Dr. Loraine Boettner puts it, "God does not stand for a policy of peace at any price, but for righteousness at any cost." If he entered the theological arena it was because necessity was laid upon him. Great things were at stake. The Church's doctrine was being corrupted; her mission hindered. The people must be alerted whatever the cost. His magazine had numerous readers throughout the Christian world, and there are many today who bless his memory for his dauntless and faithful witness. Not for self-praise did he at any time take up his pen, but for the glory of the Master Whom he loved so well.

In my early ministry in Greenock we were a great deal in each other's company, for the mutual accessibility of our congregations made us reasonably close neighbours. We travelled extensively together; we were fellow-deputies to many international and inter-denominational gatherings; we made free of each other's homes and shared each other's yoke in many ways.

Latterly, his letters betrayed that his fine mental powers were losing their grasp, and the last letter of all touched me deeply. It was written on an air mail form and quite inadequately addressed. And when I opened it, I found that the pages were blank. But when I turned it over in my hand I noticed that something was written under the sealing-flap. Very carefully, I uncovered this message: "My dear George, I cannot tell you how much your friendship has meant to me these last fifty years. Thank you for everything. Jim."

My emotions were deeply stirred by that farewell message. I confess that I wept unashamedly over that thin ribbon of blue airmail paper, yet thanked God for all the blessings He had sent me through these many years of close fellowship with one of the most Christ-like men I ever knew. Jim Grier touched many lives, especially among young people. And there was blessing in the contact. He was only one of the many with whom I became bound in ties of helpful friendship through co-operation in the medium of the Reformed Faith.

The Irish Evangelicals were warm-hearted and very appreciative of any services that the Free Church rendered to them. On one occasion, when I was in Belfast, I had an encounter with a zealous member of the Knock congregation. He came to express his appreciation of my visit. "Our friends in the Free Church have been very kind," he said, "for we've had Principal Maclcod, and Rev. R.M. Knox and Rev. Duncan Leitch and yourself. And now you have sent us Rev. George Mackay."

At the reference to Mr. Mackay his eye kindled. "You're all good preachers," he said, "but faith, there's none of you can preach like the old boy!"

I told Principal Macleod this story, to his great amusement. Somctime later, when Mr. Mackay and I were visiting him, Principal Macleod turned to me and said, "Did you ever tell Mr. Mackay the story?" "No," I replied. "I didn't want to give him a swelled head." At this Mr. Mackay became very curious. "Tell me, tell me," he said. So I repeated it. He chuckled enthusiastically over the story and wheezed between gales of laughter, "Take you that, take you that, all of you. That is a discerning man!"

Shortly afterwards he paid a very enjoyable return visit to the Irish Evangelicals.

One of the things that I took with me when I first left London to make my home in Scotland was a pen which my elder brother gave me just around that time. Compared with the variety of fountain pens in use today it was a crude implement, but in its day it registered a great advance in the art of writing. True, you had to use an awkward glass filler when charging it, and it had a nasty habit of leaking onto your fingers when you were writing with it, and of blotting your handkerchief when you restored it to your pocket, but the lad who had a fountain pen in those days was a marked person and much to be envied.

My new acquisition went immediately into service. With it I wrote home, helped my friend Duncan to maintain contact with his correspondents, wrote my monthly answers to the *Instructor Questions*, used it in my College examinations, and wrote my first article for the Church Youth Magazine.

The habit grew, and in the years that followed I wrote articles, mainly for religious periodicals.

But I had no thought of producing a book until 1935, when Dr. Stewart wrote to me suggesting I should make a series of articles that I had written for the *Monthly Record* available in more permanent form. The suggestion was backed up by Principal Macleod, and a volume of biographical histories was published, entitled *An Orchard of Pomegranates*. Similar biographies appeared in later years. At the request of the Knox Press other more historical books were published in 1943, the centenary year of the Disruption.

On the deaths of Principal Maclean, and of Principal Macleod, it was suggested to me that I should write their biographies, for both men were members of my Kirk Session. In 1940, during the Second World War, when people were asking in bewilderment "If God is a God of love, how can He allow war?" the I.V.F. invited me to submit a manuscript on the subject. I agreed and it was published, under the title *The Goodness and Severity of God*.

Over the years the collection of books and pamphlets grew, as well as contributions to a variety of evangelical publications, both in this country and overseas. These productions became the means of giving me happy contacts with Christians in various countries, helpful contacts which, in many instances, grew into close friendships and useful co-operation.

15: The Microphone Goes to Church

The advent of Religious Broadcasting was seen from the very beginning as a momentous event. Some in the Churches welcomed it; others regarded it with profound misgiving. It had a tremendous potentiality for good, but this was offset by its capacity for evil. The more conservative churches are always more cautious in their attitude to "innovations", and religious broadcasting was without doubt the greatest innovation of the century, from the Church's viewpoint. The radio transmitter might well prove to be a *Trojan Horse* in the Church.

The Free Church of Scotland was still trying to make up its mind in the matter when I made my first religious broadcast. It made it easier that it was a mid-week service, for it meant that the question of Sabbath labour did not yet arise. But it would have to be faced. Could the activity entailed in religious broadcasting on the Lord's Day be listed in the category of "works of necessity and mercy"? Some went even farther and questioned if the microphone should be given *any* place in the spreading of the Gospel. It was used in so much that was hostile to the Gospel that its use as an agency of evangelisation seemed utterly incongruous. Some even brought the Apostle James into the discussion,"Doth a fountain send forth at the same place sweet water and bitter?"

Now, it seemed obvious that very little of all this was really relevant, and, for myself, I took the view that this was a case in which Dr. John R. Mott's slogan should be applied,"Evangelise the inevitable."

Broadcasting had come to stay; let us claim it to the fullest extent for Christ and His cause. By its means we could send the message of life to people cut off by wide moorlands and stormy seas from the normal gatherings for public worship. We could reach the patient in the hospital bed and whisper in his ear a message from Christ. We could soon be reaching the remotest mission fields where so many still sat in darkness and the shadow of death. We could be setting up an agency that would transmit God's Word beyond bamboo curtains and iron curtains and every other device that might be set up by men for the hindering of the Gospel. We might be storming the citadels of error with the liberating message of Truth.

Let us indeed evangelise the inevitable!

Principal John Macleod had no doubt as to where his duty lay when in those early days of Religious Broadcasting he was invited to broadcast a Gaelic service from King's College Chapel, Aberdeen. A press-cutting which lies before me as I write recalls that the preacher "in rich sonorous tones, preached an earnest, evangelical discourse from Genesis 32:10... *Chan airidh mi air a chuid is lugha de na trocairibh sin uile no de'n fhirinn sin uile a nochd Thu do d' sheirbhiseach...*".

Mr. Neil Maclean of the B.B.C. was precentor, and Mr. Donald MacCuish, then a student, read the Scripture portion.

Probably the first service broadcast from a Free Church was one conducted by Rev. Ian MacRury M.A., then of Strathpeffer Free Church, from Garve. The first official broadcast was in 1938, from Glasgow, to commemorate the tercentenary of the famous Covenanting Assembly, held under the Moderatorship of Alexander Henderson of Leuchars, when Episcopacy was abolished, and Presbyterianism restored as the order of the Scottish Church.

The request to broadcast the service was addressed to me in the first instance, by the B.B.C., but I suggested that it be passed on to the Free Church Assembly Arrangements Committee for their consideration, so that it should have what might be regarded as a form of official backing. I also proposed that Dr. Donald Maclean might be suggested as the preacher for the occasion inasmuch as he was Retiring Moderator that year, and also Professor of Church History in the Free Church College. But Dr. Maclean would agree to conduct the service only if I preached the sermon. And that was how things were arranged.

The event did not pass without some criticism which, happily, was easy to refute. The rumour had been circulated that the B.B.C. insisted on censoring every document that they accepted for transmission — even sermon manuscripts used in Religious Broadcasts, and it was argued with some warmth that such an interference with the preaching of the Gospel simply ought not to be tolerated. The Committee fully agreed. But there was no case to answer! For, as it happened, not a single scrap of manuscript was submitted either by Dr. Maclean or myself at that service of commemoration, except, indeed, the bare order of service! And in the years that followed, although it was customary, but not obligatory, to submit copies of scripts that were to be used in Religious Broadcasting the only purpose of doing so was to secure accuracy with the timing. Never once was I asked for a script for submission to censorship of any kind.

Another adverse view on Religious Broadcasting in those early days was that it would have a detrimental effect on church-going. There was substance in the fear. There are always people around who cannot resist the appeal of novelties and gimmicks. But, with time, the fascination wears off, and it is realised that there is no substitute for the Church of Christ; no adequate alternative to the fellowship of the saints; no means of promoting spiritual fellowship comparable with the living presence. Whatever impressions you may be able to put across by means of the microphone, you can no more transmit the spirit of true worship than you can, by means of radio, broadcast the mingled perfumes of the meadow.

One thing that I have always feared, however, is the trivialising effect of the *snippetty* sermon. Dr. D.M. Lloyd-Jones has said many pithy things in this connection in his *Preaching and Preachers*. There is undoubtedly an inexcusable imbalance in the allocation of timing as between religious and non-religious broadcasting. I confess that there were times when the shorter religious broadcasts seemed rather futile. What could you do, for instance, with a mid-week service that had to be compressed into fifteen minutes, or an epilogue that had to be squeezed into three?

I spoke my thoughts to Hugh Macphee on one occasion, and in a large measure, he agreed with me. By all means let us press for more broadcasting time, but, he urged, let us use to the best effect the measure we have. And to give weight to his words he quoted the counsel of Rob Donn, the Sutherland bard, to his mother. She, good lady, was cutting the corn with her sickle, complaining as she did so of the lightness of the crop, when Rob, a mere child at the time, delivered himself of the following effusion:

> *Bi thusa dol, a null 's a nall,*
> *Gu'n ruig thu ceann na clais';*
> *'S cha-n 'eil agad air, ma tha e gann,*
> *Ach na gheibh thu ann 'thoirt as.*

> (roughly translated:
> *You just keep on from side to side,*
> *Till you come to the end of the run,*
> *And tho' it be spare, let this be your care,*
> *To take out as much as you can.*)

I changed my view, but not under the influence of the prodigious Rob.

What happened was this.

My former fellow-student, Rev. Robert J. Murray M.A., invited me to assist at his communion services at Strathy in July 1948, and, between times, took me to see an old, bed-ridden lady in his congregation, who was completely cut off from church attendance by acute arthritis.

Mr Murray's intended introduction proved quite unnecessary. She knew who I was and greeted me warmly.

"So you've met Mr. Collins before," said Mr. Murray.

"Not met, but heard," was the reply. And then, pointing to her little radio, she explained herself, "Many's the good word I've heard from him through that blessed invention," she said, "and I'm glad to have the opportunity to thank him in person."

The next time Hugh Macphee sought my help, my compliance was immediate; and I told him why. And never again, so far as I can recall, did I refuse a request from Hugh, or any of his successors, for help in this wise. Difficulties there might be, but the thought of the disabled sufferer in Strathy, and many like her, waiting so eagerly for her weekly portion, was enough to produce the extra determination to see the matter through.

The recording of sermons for broadcasting was not much in favour in those days. Artificiality, it was alleged, came into the exercise, and the listener detected it. "Be quite *natural*," our advisers used to urge us as we were about to go on the air. Excellent advice but hard to follow! How could a poor tensed-up novitiate "be quite natural" before such a pitiless, soul-less thing as a B.B.C. microphone or, later, T.V. camera that glowered at you with the fixed stare of a blood-shot eye? I remember, with abiding satisfaction, a remark made by our ex-Prime Minister, Harold MacMillan, in what must have been one of his early talks on television, when, in an allusion to the difficulty of trying to be "natural" before an unseen audience, he pointed with outstretched arm toward the T.V. camera, and exclaimed, with an amusing grimace, "I've never quite mastered the art of looking into the lens of the television camera and treating it as one of the family."

In a small way, I knew the feeling, and recalled my effort to overcome it. The occasion was a live T.V. service from the Aberdeen B.B.C. studios. I had a timing rehearsal which had the effect of filling me with dismay. I knew what was the matter. At the actual broadcast I would be preaching in an empty studio and trying at the same time to conjure up a visible audience.

I confided my feelings to Stanley Pritchard who was in charge of the service, and whom I had known for a long time. I suggested that, instead of using full manuscript, as we had done at the timing rehearsal, I should use just one small sheet of notes, and free my eyes to look through the large glass panel opposite to where some members of B.B.C. staff who were concerned with the broadcast would be doing their respective duties. They would provide the human element; they would be my "congregation"! Mr. Pritchard readily agreed, and we arranged a method whereby the time limits would be safe-guarded.

The plan worked, and Mr. Pritchard was kindly and reassuring. But what of the wider public?

One interesting answer from that source came two days later in rather cryptic terms. It was written on a postcard from Colinton Manse, and the message simply was:

Broadcast Service. $A + +$
Many thanks
W. Laing

It took me a little time to realise that the rather academic style of his assessment of the broadcast was a puckish allusion to my then recent election to the Church History Chair in the Free Church College!

I had never met Dr. Laing and appreciated his kindness all the more on that account, and also because his tribute, though so waggishly expressed, was the serious judgment of a discerning critic and might, perhaps, be humbly taken as representative of a few more!

But though I have never taken enthusiastically to T.V. Religious Broadcasting, I readily admit that it brings a new, and most valuable, dimension into the work of broadcasting the Gospel. It brings personality to the microphone. It almost humanises it. It calls both Eye and Ear to attention, and, through them, makes a strong double appeal to the emotions and affections of the heart – yes, even in a brief epilogue. This was brought home to me in a special manner when, many years ago, I was speaking to a gathering in a Knightswood Church of Scotland of which Dr. J.G.S.S. Thomson was then minister.

After the meeting a gentleman came to the church vestry to have a word with me. We were strangers to each other, but he had seen in the press Church Notices that I was to be in Glasgow that evening, and he resolved to come along and, if possible, meet me.

Shortly before then, he said, he was sitting in a room in his house, waiting for the midnight news. In an adjoining room his wife lay dying, and his world was collapsing around him. He did not think of praying, simply because he did not believe in prayer. It was nearing news-time, so he turned on his T.V. just to pass the weary moments. It was not news-time yet, but someone was speaking. It turned out to be a religious epilogue, and, though he was not interested, he just let it run on. The speaker's subject was *Rising above Things*, and he told of a flight that he had taken from Renfrew to Belfast sometime before. It was a cold, dismal, drizzly morning, he said, and when he took his seat in the plane he unfolded his newspaper and began to read. A man sitting beside him was similarly occupied.

As the plane took off and began to rise through the murky clouds there was still no improvement. And then, quite suddenly, the cabin was flooded with brilliant sunshine. They had risen above the clouds. Momentarily, his fellow-passenger looked up from his paper, and remarked, "What a change!" and then added, "You see, you can always get into the sunshine, if you rise high enough!" And the minister who was giving the epilogue, he recalled, used that experience as an illustration of his theme for the night. Yes, he insisted, we could get above things, whatever they might be, if we really sought God's help. By waiting upon Him we could renew our strength and rise up with wings like eagles, right into the sunshine and peace of His presence. And the speaker urged his hearers who might be spiritually under the weather to "wait upon the Lord" for strength to "rise above things" on wings of prayer and faith into the peace that passeth all understanding.

"It seemed like clutching at a straw," said my visitor, "but a miracle happened. I lost my wife that night, but I found my Saviour. And having heard that you were to be here this evening, I felt that I must come and tell you."

I left the meeting that night more than ever convinced that, however dissatisfied we might be with the inadequacy of the time assigned to religious broadcasting by the B.B.C., it would be wrong to refuse our co-operation just on that account. *"Gather up the fragments..."* was the Lord's charge to His disciples, and one could well relate the charge to their future ministry. In the long history of the Church He has shown us how much He can do with the *"fragments"* that men put at His disposal. Let us accept the *"fragments"* for His service, but press for more. Obviously, in a mixed and materialistic society we need not expect a ready compliance with our demand. *"What concord hath light with darkness?"*

But what can we do? Does the answer lie in part, at least, in the creation of a definitely Christian Broadcasting Service?

16: The Road to the Isles

During my boyhood and adolescent years in Sutherland my
activities were confined almost entirely to the bounds of Wester
Sutherland and Ross, and I had no strong urge to extend my
borders. What more could heart desire than what we already had?
Contentment had completely taken over. Yet, with the passing years
horizons were to widen and other places and other people were to
enrich my experience and encourage me in my pilgrimage. Amongst
the most influential of these were the beautiful islands, and the fine
people, of our Western Scottish seaboard. Let me begin a brief
account of this influence with the island which, very early in life,
first impressed its presence upon me.

1. THE ISLE OF LEWIS.

I had often heard it said that on a clear day in summer, from the
top of the *Cnoc Breac* which towers protectively over Elphin, one
could pick out with the naked eyes the east coast of Lewis. But our
clear days were not numerous; and when one *did* come, I was usually
occupied with duties on the lower levels of the world's surface.

Then, one day, it happened! I was out on the hills with my uncle
Sandy, who had his "spying-glass" slung over his shoulder. "Look,"
he said, do you see that line away on the skyline?"

To begin with, I didn't; so he pulled out his telescope and put it to
my eye and said, "Look now; that's Lewis." And that was how I had
my first glimpse of Lewis, and my first faint inkling of how "stout
Cortez" would have felt,

> *"when with eagle eyes*
> *he stared at the Pacific, and all his*
> *men*
> *Look'd at each other with a mild*
> *surmise*
> *Silent upon a peak in Darien."*

Some day, I resolved, I must visit there. But it was not until March
1932 that my ambition was realised.

The occasion was the Spring Communion in the Free Church of

Cross (Ness) where my College friend, Alexander Macleod, was then minister. There was no passenger plane service between Glasgow and Stornoway in those days, and the MacBrayne steamer *Lochness* could be depended on to test her own sea-worthiness and yours as she ploughed her resolute way from Kyle of Lochalsh to Stornoway. Blue ribands were not in her line. Her aim was not to get you there in record time, but simply to get you there.

Travel conditions from Stornoway to the more remote parts of the Island were Spartan by present-day standards. Rough, narrow roads with gaping pot-holes imposed their own speed limits, and the buses available for public transport were definitely not designed for comfort. Motor-cars were still luxuries beyond the reach of "minimum stipend" ministers, so visiting ministers for the communion seasons had usually to finish their long journey, if they came from the mainland, in a vehicle whose road-worthiness, in those pre-M.O.T. times, might well be open to question. It could well be also that some of the passengers had fortified themselves for the journey by a prolonged visit to the Stornoway pubs, thereby making themselves very undesirable companions to their fellow-travellers of more sober habits. But this did not often happen, and even when it did, the inconvenience of the journey was more than recompensed by the joy of arrival.

Ness overwhelmed me to begin with. Large though the church was, its capacity could be well taxed in those days even by the local congregation, and when this was augmented by contingents of worshippers from other parts of the island the pews became tightly packed.

It was a bitterly cold day in March 1932 when I preached my first sermon in Ness, and I was aware that in those days the church had no heating system. I looked apprehensively at Mr. Macleod when, in the vestry, he proceeded to divest himself of his heavy overcoat.

"Should I leave my coat on?" I asked him, as we were about to enter the church. "Well, perhaps you should," he replied, "but I don't think you'll need it for long." And I did not. The bulk of the congregation had already been seated for, perhaps, as much as close on half an hour, and by the time we entered the pulpit, the chill was already off the air! And when the service ended around two hours later (and that was reasonable measure in those days, and is even yet endurable) the large building was comfortably warm!

There was a glow of spiritual warmth as well. A spirit of prayer and worship permeated the whole enclosure and established a complete *rapport* between pulpit and pew. "There is nothing,"

Principal Macleod once remarked to me, "that draws me out like a Lewis Communion."

The singing of the Gaelic Psalms, under the leadership of precentors who were masters of their craft — and of some who weren't! — and the sincere praise that accompanied the exercise helped to combine heart and voice in the adoration of the Giver of all good.

Incidentally, on that visit to Ness I was put to a test that I had not expected. Mr. Donald Mackay, who was then headmaster of Lionel School, requested me to visit his school while I was in Ness, and address the pupils. When we met at the time arranged he explained that he was dividing my prospective audience into two sections — senior and junior, which would mean *two* short addresses; and, as few of the younger children knew little or any English before coming to school, my address to them had better be in Gaelic!

I think I must have winced visibly. Never before had I given a talk in Gaelic to a gathering of little children and the thought of doing so now quite shook me. But Gaelic is such a flexible and expressive language that the ordeal proved less testing than I had feared. Anyway, Mr. Mackay — probably fearing the worst — told them in his introductory words that when I first went to school, and for some years thereafter, I had no Gaelic. That revelation of my ignorance probably stirred their curiosity and secured for me their sympathetic interest. It struck me as good psychology!

That visit to Lewis was the first of many. Several of my fellow-students, most of them my seniors, had taken pastorates in the island. Others were to follow, and the succession was continued by some of my own students. Lewis manses have been to me homes from homes in the kindliest sense.

And if the human race has ever produced kindlier people than those who inhabit the Long Island, I have yet to find them.

Still on this theme, another visit to Ness comes to mind.

By this time, another friend of College days — Rev. John M. Morrison — was minister of Ness, and we were both to go to Stornoway after the Ness communion in March — Mr. Morrison to proceed overnight to Mallaig, and then on to Fort William, and I to nearby Kinloch to assist Rev. Murdoch Macrae at his communion. But a wild blizzard blew up, and by the time we were due to leave, the road to Stornoway had become well-nigh blocked. Our bus driver reckoned he would just be able to make it, but at one point, a low- slung van got stuck in the snow just ahead of us. And that was that! The prospect was that we should have to spend the night in the stranded bus, but John thought it better to set off back to his manse on foot. So off we went, with the storm swirling around us. High winds whipped up the snow into a dense flurry, and then, by way of climatic variety, subjected us to a perfect fusillade of the largest hailstones I had ever seen, and that struck like bullets.

It so happened that I had taken a tartan travelling rug with me when I set out for Lewis on that occasion — the only time I had ever done so. We wrapped it around our heads and shoulders for protection from the blizzard, and with linked arms, battled on.

But by the time we reached the township of Galson we began to talk about looking for shelter somewhere for the rest of the night, for it was now around midnight. While we were talking, we suddenly descried a light shining out through the stormy darkness. It came from a window; and, as we approached, a voice reached us, *"Nach tig sibh a stigh? Bha sinn a feitheamh ribh."* ("Will you not come in? We were waiting for you.")

But how did they know about us?

The owner of the stranded bus, good, kind John Mitchell, had been trying to locate his lost vehicle by checking up on certain phone-points along the route. Our rescuers were able to inform him that it had passed their house en route for Stornoway, and he was able to inform them that it had not even reached Barvas. Suspecting that some of the stranded passengers might try to walk back to safety, our hosts, who turned out to be the local schoolmaster and his wife, Mr. and Mrs. MacArthur, had stirred up the embers of the peat fire and made ready a guest-room lest it should be needed.

Human kindness could hardly have been more deeply appreciated. A hot meal, a refreshing bath, a warm bed; and soon we were in dreamless slumber.

It turned out that the blizzard was a freak one, affecting the northern part of the island only. Stornoway and the south were clear of the deep snow-drifts which had halted all vehicular movement in the north. Another day passed before we were able to continue our journey. This time, we got through, John to board the *Loch Seaforth* for a tranquil crossing to Mallaig, and I to be quickly transported by Murdoch Macrae to his cosy manse in Kinloch. And as I lay awake for a little that night, and reviewed the events of recent days they drew together to leave with me thoughts of the prevenient God, Who had gone before us, preparing our way, and bringing us safely to journey's end. And when the pilgrimage of life is ending, and the light of the Father's House breaks through the murk of the valley, may it be given us to hear the welcoming voice over the distance, "Won't you come in? I'm ready for you." And His preparation will leave nothing more to be desired.

The Highlands of Scotland, and especially the Western Isles, have still retained a sufficient residue of their hard-won heritage to preserve an ethos, a way of life, that is distinctly Christian, though the pressures of secularism make their presence increasingly felt.

The historic Communion services of the Scottish Presbyterian Churches are still carefully planned and regularly observed events. Beginning on a Thursday, which was specially assigned to humiliation and confession of sin, there followed a daily progression of meetings for self-examination, Christian fellowship, and self-preparation — all leading to the dispensation of the Lord's Supper on the Sabbath morning; a call to the unconverted on the Sabbath evening, concluding on Monday with a service, or services, for thanksgiving.

2. UIST AND ARRAN.

I well recall the first Communion Season that I spent on the island of Grimsay, North Uist, in my early ministry. I arrived there on the Wednesday afternoon, and found the fishermen making for harbour to lay up their boats until the Communion was over. The weather was perfect and well-suited to their employment, and the fishing was good. But the most important thing that was to take place during these days was the preaching of the Word of God, and it was given its due place. And this seeking of the Kingdom of God and His righteousness was rewarded with the fulfilment of the promise, *"all other things shall be added to you."*

The Western Isles of Scotland have, over the centuries, provided a succession of able and godly ministers for the work of the church in this country, and indeed, throughout the world. Some of my closest friends of student days were from Lewis — Murdo Macrae, John M. Morrison, Duncan Morrison, Alexander Macleod, Angus Finlayson, John Mackenzie, and Murdoch Campbell — and it is to their credit, far more than to mine, that the friendship of our youth ripened with the passing years. My pilgrimage has been made lonelier by their removal, but they brought an imperishable richness to my life that has left me forever in their debt.

Some of the good elders in the pew were much more discerning hearers of the Word than a few of the preachers, who, pressed into service in the exigencies of the Post-Union days, were not always so well-grounded in theology as were their hearers.

One of the local elders on the Isle of Arran, Alexander Robertson, "Sandy Valdy", of Shiskine, was noticeable in this respect. He seldom could be prevailed upon to take a service, but he acted as precentor, and was a stickler for sound doctrine and purity of worship.

A weekend visitor who took the Sabbath services on one occasion was so satisfied with his own performance that when he came to making the intimations at the end of the service, he gushed, "My dear friends, I cannot tell how much I have enjoyed being with you today! The only thing that could have been better was the congregational singing. But the next time I come I'll bring my accordion!"

Up rose Sandy from his seat in front of the pulpit! He had not enjoyed the sermon and the intimation was too much. Turning to the preacher he replied, "For you, Sir, there will be no next time!" — and there wasn't!

3. SKYE.

It was at the request of Rev. Donald Mackinnon of Portree that I first visited the Isle of Skye. Donald had been a teacher before entering the ministry of the Church and, on completing his theological studies in 1923, had become the first Free Church minister of Portree after the Church Union of 1900. Building again from the very foundations, he had gathered around him the nucleus of a loyal charge before moving to Kennoway Free Church in 1943. Donald was a true Highlander whose loyalty to the *Misty Isle* never flagged, notwithstanding that the rest of his ministry was given to Fife.

A thoroughly competent Gaelic scholar and reliable genealogist, his services were always in requisition by students of clan history, and research scholars. He was an authority on Flora Macdonald and the Jacobite Rising under Prince Charles Edward Stuart in 1745.

Dame Flora Macleod of Dunvegan Castle enlisted him as her editor for the Clan Macleod Magazine, and saw to it that she kept him supplied with nominees whom she regarded as qualifying for enrolment among her clan. When I disclosed to her, on meeting her at Dunvegan on one occasion, that Macleod blood ran in my veins, the immediate and almost obvious effect was that I had added a cubit to my stature! The incident was almost immediately followed by a letter from the Castle requesting information about myself for inclusion, with my name, in her Clan Records for the Macleods. I respectfully declined the proposed honour, explaining that I was born a Londoner, the son of an English father, from whom I took my surname.

But Dame Flora was not easily thwarted! Back came a letter reminding me that, in the old Clan system, the descent was reckoned by matriarchate, not the patriarchate, for the good reason that every man contains more of his mother's blood than of his father's! Cogent though the argument was, it failed of its purpose!

Donald Mackinnon, however, is better remembered as an ambassador of Christ than as a clan historian, and some of his contributions to Gaelic literature are stamped with an erudition, and bear an evangelical warmth, that makes them acceptable still to a wide spectrum of Gaelic readers.

Skye had lain under the spiritual blight of Moderatism for many years, but had shared in the widespread renewal of blessing that led up to the Disruption of 1843. The great leader of the Evangelicals in that stirring period was Dr. Roderick Macleod of Snizort, whose name exhales a lingering fragrance in Skye to this day.

I still recall a strange and somewhat disturbing relic of his ministry that I encountered in my first visit to his famous church in Snizort. A friend of College days, the Rev. Malcolm Macleod, was then minister of the congregation. The manse had fallen into grave disrepair, and brave efforts were being made to restore it. Some things, quite obviously, had gone beyond service, and, in the prevailing financial stringency, it was decided to remove them. But there was one thing that they decided, after much thought and discussion, must not be removed. Mr. Macleod conducted me personally to my bedroom to give me an explanation which he thought was due. Pointing to a large iron ring which hung from the ceiling above my pillow, he identified it as a device provided for Dr. Macleod whereby in his declining years, he could pull himself up in bed when he wanted to change his position.

I was glad of the explanation, for the odd accessory could well suggest a more sinister purpose! There had been a suggestion to remove it, but tangible memorials of *Maighstir Ruairidh* (Mister Roderick) were becoming rare. So the ring was tolerated.

The fine solid manse has had a far more extensive refurbishing in more recent times, and the old iron ring has disappeared from its former location, but I strongly suspect that its present whereabouts are still well known. But what matter? *Maighstir Ruairidh's* most enduring memorials consist of the rich crop of converts whose changed lives won for him the designation *The Apostle of Skye*, as the minister whose work did more for the spread of the Gospel in his native Isle than that of any of his contemporaries.

The after-gleanings of this rich harvest were still in clear evidence in Skye when I first visited the island, and to meet in the various congregations some of the older people who could testify to having received blessing from Dr. Macleod's ministry was an enriching experience.

Prominent among the notable Skye Christians of my acquaintance was John Ross of Kilmaluag. John's prominence was not due to any outstanding gifts, but to his sheer weight of godliness and entire devotion to the cause of Christ.

He spent some of his early life in the heavy industries on Clydeside, and a narrow escape from death that he had there when a heavy piece of machinery fell within inches of where he was standing, was used by God to impress upon him "the littleness of time and the greatness of eternity", as Chalmers would have it.

John was early called to serve his church in the Home Mission Field and he soon became a favourite with the congregations to whom he ministered. Occasionally "a word in the other language" was desirable, when it was known that certain visitors did not understand the Gaelic. John had no hesitation in trying out his English when the occasion demanded. This was sometimes an embarrassment to his own friends. After one such occasion, a daughter remonstrated with her father on his grammatical mistakes. "Father," she said, "you shouldn't be attempting to preach in English — for one thing you have not the grammar." John, however, did not regard that as too serious an impediment. "*Och, a nighean,*" was the answer, "*chan eil an Soisgeul ag iarraidh grammar ann.*" ("Och, lassie, the gospel doesn't need grammar at all!")

John's ventures into English were sometimes even more amusing. On one occasion a local doctor, seeing him on the road ahead, stopped to offer him a lift. When their destination was reached, John warmly thanked the doctor in these words, "Thank you, thank you, doctor. I'm sorry to be bothered with you!"

My first meeting with John was at a Communion service in Uig. He referred to it when I visited him on his deathbed many years later. "Do you remember," he asked, "the text that you had on that occasion?" I told him I didn't. He immediately replied, "It was on the Pharisee and the Publican in Luke chapter 18, and especially the Publican's prayer, *God be merciful to me, a sinner.*"

Having quoted the text John was silent for a moment, and then he remarked, "Do you know, that was the first real prayer I ever offered?"

Not that John was a stranger to formal prayer; but looking back it seemed to him that he had never offered sincere prayer until the Holy Spirit had revealed his deepest need to him at the throne of grace. "And I suppose, John," I said, "that you will find these words suitable on many occasions still." To which he gravely replied. "Many's the time I've used them since. I'm now on my deathbed and *they suit me still.*" That was true spiritual insight; "God, be merciful to me a sinner" is always, and everywhere, an appropriate petition.

4. THE ISLANDS OF ARGYLL.

It was in the month of November 1929 that I first set foot on the islands of Argyll. I had been at Oban early in the month assisting Rev. A.M. Ross at his winter communion there, and had included a visit to the lovely island of Kerrera while there. The Free Church congregation in Tobermory, Mull, was vacant at the time, and, in his capacity as interim-moderator in charge of the vacancy, Mr. Ross extracted a promise from me that I would return later in the month to take the communion services there. So it came about that on the Fast Day of the communion week that winter, I was sitting in the window of a comfortable little hotel, chatting with an old elder who had kindly come along to keep me company between the services. It was an amazingly good day for the time of the year. The waters of the beautiful bay were placid and calm. The mountains of Morven were darkly silhouetted against the wan blue of the distant horizon. The town was beginning its hibernation after the bustle of a busy tourist season, and the shops were closed for the Fast Day holiday. Peace reigned supreme.

Inevitably, we had been talking about the Spanish Armada gold reputedly buried in the silt of the bay, and, in particular, the many costly and unrewarding efforts which had been made to retrieve it, when, suddenly, we heard a voice in the distance singing sweetly some verses that seemed familiar and that we recognised from the tune before the words could be distinguished. They were:

> *When He cometh, when He cometh*
> *To make up His jewels,*
> *All His jewels, precious jewels*
> *His loved and His own,*

Like the stars of the morning
His bright crown adorning
They shall shine in their beauty,
Bright gems for His crown.

We looked along the almost deserted street and identified the singer as a teenaged girl giving, we hoped, expression to a conviction and personally held expectation. At all events, we were struck by the coincidence that while we had been talking about treasure hunts that had failed she had been singing about a quest that had partially succeeded already, and would be crowned with complete success in God's fixed time.

It was G.F. Roots' believing response to God's own promise through the prophet Malachi. "*... they shall be mine, saith the Lord, in that day when I make up my jewels, and I will spare them, as a man spareth his own son that serveth him...*" And we have Jesus' own reassurance, "*They shall never perish, neither shall any man pluck them out of my hand.*"

Generally, the evangelist's pulse was not vigorous in those days, but Argyll has its own Evangelical traditions, and they are of a high order. St. Columba and his fellow-missionaries were men of high endeavour, and pioneer evangelists of great foresight and sound judgment. In choosing Iona as their centre they availed themselves of several important advantages. The girdling waters of their island home teemed with fish of various kinds. Its fields were fertile, by West Highland standards, and the nearby and larger island of Tiree always seemed to have "*bread enough and to spare.*" It would appear therefore that the community was economically self-sustaining.

And there were helpful affinities. In the middle of the fifth century AD Dalriadic Scots from Northern Ireland had been settling in the territory which became known as the *Kingdom of Dalriada*, the area equivalent to the modern Argyllshire. St. Columba and his companions came to Iona in 563 to people of the same blood as themselves, and Conall, the king of the Scottish Dalriadic kingdom, was a kinsman of St. Columba. The links between the two Dalriadas were never severed, and intercourse between the two communities was facilitated by their nearness to each other. Moreover, the immigrant evangelists were good seamen and masters of their coracles. With these they could sail up the waters of the deeply indented coasts and narrow straits of the West to evangelise new areas and to maintain communications between the various abbeys and other ecclesiastical settlements as these arose.

Iona is indeed a place where it is easy for Scottish Christians to see visions and dream dreams; I doubt indeed if there is a better. While one does not readily share Boswell's extravagant admiration for Dr. Samuel Johnson, the acknowledgment will be made without grudging that the irascible lexicographer could sometimes say a fine thing finely, and certainly, his words, inscribed on a tablet at the roadside in Iona, are worthy of the enduring prominence thus accorded them:

That man is little to be envied whose patriotism would not gain force upon the plain of Marathon, or whose piety would not grow warmer among the ruins of Iona.

But the restored buildings in Iona, as well as those that are still left as ruins, have much less connection with Columba than most visitors imagine. There was nothing like them in the island for long after St. Columba's time; they belong rather to the period when the rustic simplicity of the Columban settlement had given way to the more elaborate pattern of Roman usage.

The present-day buildings have very little significance for us today other than to mark the site of the original colony of wood and wattle huts that housed the pioneers of the Columban Church in Scotland. Central to this area is *Tor-Abb* (The Abbot's Mound), so called because it is identified as the hillock where Columba had his cell, and from which he could easily exercise an oversight of the whole community. His "bed" is shown as a slab of rock; and his "pillow" a stone, now carefully engraved, is safely housed within the museum nearby. St. Oran, the first of St. Columba's followers to die in Iona, has given his name to the ancient burial-ground where many Kings of Scotland, Ireland and Norway are interred in an enclosure called "*The Ridge of the Kings.*"

I had dearly wanted to be unrecognised on my visit to Iona, just to ward off requests for service. I certainly was not well-known in the district, but I was determined to give no clues. I had had a very busy summer and felt the need of this short break before taking up the duties of the new Session. In my correspondence regarding my bookings in the St. Columba Hotel therefore, I used no clerical titles, and when, in due time, I set out for Iona I avoided the use of clerical attire. But one moment of imprudence destroyed my plan. I reached Iona early on a Saturday afternoon and, over a cup of tea, I asked Mr. Walters of the Columba Hotel where one might find a place of worship the following day. There was just one Church service, he replied, and it would be held in the Church of Scotland. When, as a supplementary question, I asked if Dr. Sinton was still there, mine host replied, "Oh, so you know Dr. Sinton. Yes, he is still here." I knew that my attempts at achieving anonymity were in danger of frustration.

"No," I replied, "I just happened to meet him once at the funeral of a member of his last congregation."

But before the evening was out, Dr. Sinton was across to see me. Mr. Walters had told him that I was there, and he had remembered our former meeting. It was a pleasant encounter, but it had the consequence I had planned to avoid. It was the month of September, and Iona's tourist accommodation was still fully taxed, and, for lack of an evening church service a request was made to me that I should conduct a service in the lounge of the hotel. I agreed; but later in the afternoon Mr. Walters was back to say that, in addition to hotel guests, several people from the village had expressed the desire to attend, and to have the service in the Abbey; there would be no difficulty in obtaining the use of it even at such short notice. It was explained that, by agreement with the Duke of Argyll, the building was made available to all the Scottish Reformed denominations who might desire to worship there if it was available. So, at the agreed hour a mixed inter-denominational and international gathering assembled themselves in a simple act of worship in the building on the historic site where St. Columba and his devoted fellow-missionaries planned for the conversion of Scotland.

Later that evening, Mr Walters brought me a request that we should hold a meeting for prayer and fellowship on each of the remaining evenings of my stay in the island and meeting, as we did, in the St. Oran's Chapel — named, like the burial ground already mentioned, after the first member of the Columban team of missionaries to die, and be buried, in the island.

I got my "rest" in Iona, and though it was not of the kind that I had planned for myself I did not regret it. It was rest in Christian fellowship − the rest of spiritual renewal.

17: With the Fathers and Brethren

The time-honoured way of addressing the supreme Court of the Church is a standing reminder of the relationship which the office-bearers of the Church sustain to each other. As members of the Church, they were *brethren*. Among them were some who had long borne "the burden and heat of the day", thereby acquiring the valuable experience that produces the accumulated wisdom of the years. Appeals are often directed to them for guidance when unforeseen difficulties are encountered, and thus one age endows another, and God maintains the continuity of His Church.

The first General Assembly that I ever attended was the Inverness Assembly of 1922. Thirty-four years previously there had been a very special Assembly of the Free Church in the Highland capital. The move for Union with the United Presbyterians was running into difficulty in the Highlands, for the anti-Union party were almost all in that area, or of Highland extraction, and they were appealing to the people for loyalty to the old standards. Their success in this effort caused the Union party considerable concern, and it was this fact that led to the holding of the Inverness Assembly in 1888. To give its deliberations greater weight in the North, a popular Highland minister, Dr. Gustavus Aird of Creich, was elected Moderator.

Inverness Town Council showed its appreciation of the Assembly's presence among them by holding a civic reception in honour of the event, and conferring the Freedom of the Burgh upon the Moderator. Large public meetings were held, and some of the best-known and most highly revered ministers of the Church were brought to the platform. Everything was done to suggest that the Free Church would be carrying its distinctive testimony intact into the United Free Church in spite of all that the Constitutionalist objectors were saying to the contrary.

Later, and in pursuance of this same policy, a Convention for the deepening of spiritual life in the Highlands was held in Inverness. This was in 1898, and again, trusted speakers from the Evangelical side were selected, and it was pre-arranged that the matters which were agitating the Church at the time should not be discussed. The aim was to represent the pro-Union majority as unchanged in their doctrinal loyalty, notwithstanding that they were moving for union with a denomination which had already modified its testimony to suit the spirit of the age.

This unusual concentration of interest in the spiritual well-being of the Church in the Highlands, while it allayed the fears of some of the people, had the undesired effect of arousing the suspicions of others — especially those who recognised the Free Church Declaratory Act of 1892 as a subtle means of moving away from the Westminster Confession of Faith without openly repudiating it.

The Free Church General Assembly which met in Inverness in 1922 was numerically insignificant as compared with the pre-Union Assembly of 1888. But the membership gathered sufficient strength to demonstrate the unreliability of the United Free prophets who had predicted for the continuing Free Church a life-span of five years!

There was indeed no indication of advancing decrepitude in the Reports submitted to the General Assembly. A number of ministers, and a few congregations that had entered the United Free Church in 1900 had returned to their former loyalty, and it was evident that the Church was facing the future with courage and hope.

To some dear souls, however, the Assembly was a profound disappointment. The Church gatherings to which they were accustomed were mostly communion services, and the idea formed of a General Assembly by some of the uninitiated seemed to be a kind of super-communion season, with an unusual number of ministers and elders in attendance for a whole week, during which there would be a constant stream of theological discussion and preaching. The disillusionment was shattering! To hear men of God giving so much of their time to discussing such worldly things as Education, Industry, Economics and Politics – and even disagreeing with each other! Surely such things ought not to be!

One of the disappointed visitors, who had come a long way to that Assembly, when asked on his return home how he had enjoyed the Assembly, let himself go. "Enjoyed it? Who would enjoy *yon*? If *yon*'s what an Assembly is like it's no' me that will bother to go to another, not even if they met doon the road from me."

There have been times when many of the participants themselves have felt the same! But they kept going. And at the closing session they have sung together, by time-honoured custom, the words of Psalm 122:

> *Now, for my friends' and brethren's sakes*
> *Peace be in thee, I'll say.*

And for the house of God our Lord,
I'll seek thy good alway.

And so it goes from year to year, the Lord using faulty instruments for the furtherance of His faultless work until His purpose is accomplished and His own Name thereby glorified.

The Retiring Moderator of the 1922 Assembly was Rev. Roderick Macleod B.D. of Knock, Lewis. Mr. Macleod — a native of Harris — had been ordained to the ministry in the Canadian Presbyterian Church, but had returned to Scotland in 1908 to join his brethren in the remaining Free Church in their efforts to re-man their pulpits after the depletion caused by the division of 1900. He was my predecessor, at three places removed, in my first charge, but his stay in Greenock was not of long duration, for within two years he accepted a call to the large congregation of Knock. He later returned to Clydeside as minister of Dunoon Free Church, and thus became my nearest co-presbyter across the water. At his best, he was an excellent preacher, and a helpful neighbour. His successor in the Moderatorship was Rev. Norman Campbell M.A. of Dingwall, who had succeeded Dr. Aird in Creich in 1898. He had held Creich for the Free Church in 1900, and, in 1908, had been translated to the pulpit of the even more illustrious Dr. John Kennedy of Dingwall, where he remained for the rest of his long ministry. Mr. Campbell was a front rank evangelist and he had a fruitful itinerant ministry throughout the Highlands.

Assembly eloquence has fallen upon evil days, and little is left of the oral wizardry of bygone years. But even in the attenuated Assembly of 1922 there were still several speakers who could win and hold the attention of their hearers by the sheer quality of their gifts of communication. Professor C.A. Bannatyne had passed from the scene before my student days in Edinburgh, but his surviving contemporaries always spoke of his remarkable clarity of thought, the logicality of his reasoning and his mastery of English style.

Professor J. Kennedy Cameron, as an ecclesiastic, was in a class by himself. "A good lawyer wasted," was the comment of a legal member of the Government's Executive Commission, on hearing him presenting the case of the Free Church before that body in the post-1900 discussions. As Principal Clerk of Assembly he set a standard that would be difficult to surpass. His urbanity and imperturbability gave him advantages in debate that many coveted.

Principal J.D. McCulloch's interventions in Assembly

discussions were always listened to with deep respect, for he was a man of natural dignity and gracious bearing, who always thought before he spoke, and weighed his words before he uttered them. I well recall my first meeting with him. I had been appointed as a student to take the two main services in Hope Street, Glasgow, Free Church on the first Sabbath in February 1924, and had dreaded having him in the congregation. But a hurried survey of my hearers led me to conclude that he was not present, and my courage returned! I was well into my sermon before I detected his distinguishing white, dun-dreary whiskers in a seat under the gallery on my right. It was my undoing! It is doubtful if ever in the history of preaching was a sermon brought to such an abrupt conclusion! It was only after I got to know him well that I realised how wrong I had been about him, for a more generous and appreciative hearer it would be hard to find.

Prominent among the pre-1900 elders who had continued with the Free Church were Mr. Archibald MacNeilage and Mr. W. Rounsfell Brown B.L., both of them elders in Milton Free Church, Glasgow. They were alike men of acumen and business capacity, and they rendered voluminous service to the Church in the years of recovery after 1900. Mr. Rounsfell Brown became General Treasurer for a time, and Mr. MacNeilage — an accomplished journalist — became editor of the Free Church *Monthly Record*. Another outstanding elder in those days of rehabilitation was Mr. D. M. Smith W.S., who, for many years, served the Church as Convener of the Finance, Law and Advisory Committee. Mr. Smith's platform-gifts were not as outstanding as those of Mr. MacNeilage and Colonel Rounsfell Brown were, but he stood high in his own profession and was well known as a helper of many good causes.

Mr. MacNeilage's fiery eloquence was arresting, and his championship of a cause was often influential in rallying the undecided. His brother, John, a Glasgow printer and bookseller — who later became minister in Dunbeath, Caithness — was also an able and convincing speaker, and a man who wielded a facile pen. Archibald and he were often on opposite sides in Assembly debates, but their differences of opinion were never allowed to strain their brotherly relations.

Archibald was by far the more colourful of the two, and more than once he was approached by representatives of Parliamentary constituencies with a strongly-urged proposal that he should make himself available in political circles; but in vain. There was probably no elder of importance in the pre-1900 Free Church Assemblies whose siding with the minority was more regretted by Principal Rainy than his. Yet, though on opposite sides in what became a long and bitter conflict, these men regarded each other with high esteem, and were generous in tribute to each other even in the heat of the conflict. Each respected the other as an opponent worthy of his steel.

Mr. MacNeilage was a competent exponent of historical theology. For several years he conducted a Bible-class in Milton Free Church. Professor Duncan Blair, of the Chair of Anatomy in Glasgow University, was only one of the younger men of note who testified to the spiritual benefit they had received under his tuition, "Any theology I have," Professor Blair once remarked to me, "I owe mainly to Archibald MacNeilage's lectures on the Shorter Catechism and the Westminster Confession of Faith."

In former years the sittings of the General Assembly covered six days instead of the present four, and special preachers were appointed to officiate in the Assembly Hall on the Assembly Sabbath. The forenoon preacher was directed to draw attention in his sermon to the distinctive testimony of the Free Church of Scotland; and the evening preacher was expected to deal with some aspect of the Church's obligation to its young people.

Sometimes a young preacher became too conscious of his audience on these occasions. I recall one ingenious sermon that I heard in this connection. The text was Isaiah 53:1, "Who hath believed our report...?", and it was treated under three headings:

1. A Report Submitted
2. An Amendment Moved
3. A Deliverance Eventually Carried

Topical, perhaps, but verging on the ludicrous!

The compressing of the Assembly into four days became an economic necessity, but a regrettable one, particularly because it entailed the discontinuance of these special services, which were usually of very high quality.

After the Union of the Church of Scotland with the majority of the United Free Church in 1929 it became customary for the Lord High Commissioner to pay a courtesy visit to the Free Church General Assembly. The office of this dignitary is of long standing and is more significant than is generally known.

The Reformed Church in Scotland held its first General Assembly in 1560 and from the beginning was regarded with suspicion by the Queen's party, for John Knox and his fellow-Reformers maintained that Christ, the Head of both Church and State, had appointed a government in each of these complementary dominions, the Church exercising the spiritual jurisdiction and the State the temporal Sovereignty. Neither was to encroach upon the prerogatives of the other, but both were to co-operate in the cause of justice and righteousness under the supreme Headship of Jesus Christ, by whom *"kings reign and princes decree Justice."*

Too often, however, the relationship that developed between these two bodies was not one of co-operation but of rivalry; the Church, as in the Roman Catholic ascendancy, usurping the prerogatives of the State; and the State, on its part (as in the time of the "Bishops' Wars") encroaching upon the prerogatives of the Church.

When, therefore, the Reformed Church in Scotland set up her General Assembly, the Queen's secretary, Maitland of Lethington, questioned "whether the Queen alloweth such conventions", lest they should develop on rebellious lines. John Knox, in proof of their good faith, invited the Queen to send a personal representative to all their Assemblies. Thus originated the office of Lord High Commissioner.

After the Scottish Church Union of 1929, the remanent United Free Church took up the Voluntary stance in the matter of Church and State relation, which meant that a visit from the Sovereign's representative would no longer be appreciated. Along with that, the United Free Church General Assembly no longer synchronised with the Church of Scotland Assembly, nor did it always meet in Edinburgh. The proposal was therefore made that the Lord High Commissioner should visit the Free Church General Assembly instead, and the Free Church, consistently with her acceptance of the Establishment Principle, cordially agreed. Prior to 1929, however, the right to call the next General Assembly was vested in the Sovereign's representative, but from that time, the right of proclamation of next meeting was transferred to the Moderator, so that now, instead of the Sovereign intimating to the Assembly the Royal will regarding the date of its next meeting, through the Lord High Commissioner, it is the Assembly who, through the Moderator, intimates to the Lord High Commissioner, for notification to the Sovereign, the date which *they* have appointed for the next meeting.

The Lord High Commissioner, it may be noted, during his term of office, takes precedence of the Dukes of Scotland, and ranks next to the Lord Chancellor of Great Britain; but the dignity carries little significance nowadays.

With the passing of the years the appointments to the office came to reflect the politics of the Government of the day, with some interesting and beneficial consequences. No longer was the office to be regarded as the exclusive perquisite of the aristocracy; the commoner was given his due place.

The distinction of being the first commoner to hold this office fell to James Brown M.P., a highly respected member of the Labour party, and a pillar of the Kirk in Annbank, Ayrshire. He was a man of decidedly evangelical persuasion. The Labour party early broke with the Scottish tradition of abstaining from political activities on the Lord's Day, but James Brown could never be induced to go along with the innovationists. During my ministry in Greenock our local Lord's Day Observance Society enlisted his help at our public meetings, and he always struck the right note. In his miner days in Ayrshire he had formed a Bible Class in the Annbank congregation, and even after his election to Parliament he continued to hold it, travelling home every Friday afternoon of the Parliamentary sittings so as to be with his young people on the Sabbath.

If the appointment of Mr. Brown as Lord High Commissioner was regarded with misgiving by some, both in Parliament and in the Church, their fears were proved groundless, and the final verdict was that he magnified his office. He saw the odd side of it that he, a former miner, should receive royal honours, and dwell in the royal Palace of Holyroodhouse in Edinburgh during the Assembly, but he maintained his status with simple and natural dignity. Mrs. Brown, with her keen sense of humour, saw the funny side of the arrangement, that she should leave the simplicity of her Ayrshire home to dwell, for the duration of the Assembly, in the Palace, waited on by some of the most noble ladies in the land.

"Would you be surprised to meet Mary Queen of Scots here?" asked the Marchioness of Ailsa, as she conducted her through the corridors of the older part of the Palace. Mrs. Brown chuckled. "Mebbe," she replied, "but no' near as *she* would be to meet *me* here."

The democratising of the office of Lord High Commissioner, and the confining of the appointment to men who were elders of the Church or prominent in Christian service, was all to the good; for it undoubtedly helped to bring the Church nearer to the people. Two of the most notable Lord High Commissioners were sons of the Manse, and both had a thoroughly evangelical background and could speak with first-hand knowledge of the Church's work.

One of these was John Buchan — later to become Lord

Tweedsmuir, Governor General of Canada. Buchan knew the faith of his talented father, and the robust evangelicalism of the group to which he belonged. "In prosperous times," he said in his address to the Free Church Assembly, "when people felt comfortable and optimistic, and they were settled, there was a danger of dogmas being blurred, and distinctions — even vital distinctions – being smoothed away; but in a time of crisis, people returned to the essentials. Sands might be all very well when the sea was calm, but during a storm they wanted the rock. The creed of Calvinism was born in a time of crisis. One of the most remarkable things of our time," he added, "was the revival of the Calvinism of our forefathers."

In lighter mood, he recalled that he had "received corporal punishment at the hands of Dr. Begg because he (John Buchan) had disturbed his evening meditations." With the worthy Dr. there was no respect of persons!

Lord Tweedsmuir might have recalled how he came under the displeasure of another leading Churchman in later times.

Being in Edinburgh one weekend after his rise to fame, Buchan decided to call on Dr. David Hay Fleming who had acquired a deserved reputation as an outstanding historian of the Scottish Reformation. But when Buchan announced himself at Dr. Fleming's home he noticed that the doctor's housekeeper looked rather uneasy.

"Is there something wrong?" he asked, "Is Dr. Fleming unwell?"

"No, sir," she replied, "but he does not usually receive visitors on the Lord's Day."

"Will you please give him my card," said Buchan, "and see if he will kindly do me this favour?"

But the housekeeper knew her master. She was back immediately. "Dr. Hay Fleming presents his compliments, sir," she said, "and assures Colonel Buchan that he will be delighted to see him at his convenience tomorrow afternoon; but he does not receive callers on the Lord's Day except in an emergency."

Buchan thought none the less of Hay Fleming for his loyalty to conviction. The visit was eagerly paid the next day and mutually appreciated. Buchan had a great time in Hay Fleming's library, and then remarked teasingly, "I see, Dr. Hay Fleming, that you don't have a fiction section."

"Oh," came the reply, "but did you not notice? I have made a beginning. *There is your Montrose!*"

And they parted as firm friends!

The other son of a Free Church manse whom I referred to as having been appointed Lord High Commissioner was John Reith, who also rose high in industry and politics. His father, Dr. George Reith, the gifted minister of the College Free Church, Glasgow, had taught John to fear the Lord from his youth, and the influence of his early upbringing kept revealing itself throughout his brilliant, though often erratic, career. His address to the students of Glasgow University, as Lord Rector, was memorable. The noisy barracking that is the almost invariable accompaniment of these lectures faded into silence as Reith spoke; and the audience, as one reporter put it, "might have been a congregation gathered for worship in a great Cathedral, instead of a gathering of students out for a 'rag'."

Reith's efforts to run the B.B.C. on lines of Christian morality were the sincere endeavour of a Christian statesman to preserve the spiritual heritage which he himself valued so highly. A man of formidable appearance and of overweening ambition, capable of deep resentment which, too often, expressed itself in pungent speech, his diaries reveal the other side of his nature – especially when he writes of his father. His reference in our Assembly to his last visit to his father, just after his appointment as Governor of the B.B.C., touched a responsive chord with the "Fathers and Brethren".

As he was leaving his father's sick-room, his father, he recalled, had given him a last word of counsel. Quoting the words of Christ to His disciples, "without me ye can do nothing", he added, "Remember that, John; without Christ you can do nothing."

He made another reference to his father when he came back the following year. Alluding to the world-wide turbulence of the times, he spoke of Christ's power to control and quell it all. And then he quoted, "Perhaps the winds that have made these waves to surge and swell are but the breath of the Spirit of that Jesus Christ who is the same yesterday, today and for ever." That quotation, he then revealed, was from a sermon preached at the General Assembly of the Free Church of Scotland eighty years before. And the preacher was his father.

The emotion with which Lord Reith recalled those words strongly suggested his complete agreement with them still.

Other distinguished Commissioners whose courtesy visits to us were specially welcome were Lord Ballantrae, General Sir Richard O'Connor, and Admiral Lord Cunningham — all of them Christian leaders whose names are indelibly inscribed on our nation's roll of honour as men raised by God in a time of grave crisis to break a pagan tyranny that threatened to destroy civilisation throughout the whole world.

On rare occasions the Sovereign's representative comes from the Royal family itself. The first of these to visit the Free Church Assembly was the Duke of Kent who met his death in a plane crash on the Caithness hills during the Second World War. Prince George was looked on as perhaps the ablest member of the Royal house, and his charming wife, Princess Marina, was everywhere regarded as a lady whose life bore the clear impress of the Gospel.

The next of the Royal Commissioners was the Duke of Gloucester, who came in 1949, and again in 1963. Although not impressive as a public speaker, the Duke could emerge from his dispositional shyness in the less formal surroundings of the drawing-room of the Palace of Holyroodhouse and become a genial host, obviously helped by his accomplished wife, the Princess Alice, a daughter of the Duke of Buccleuch.

On two occasions the Queen came in person, accompanied by her Consort, Prince Philip. From the time of her coming of age when, as Princess Elizabeth, she so earnestly dedicated herself to the service of God and the nation, the people had taken her to their hearts, and cherished great expectations of her, little knowing how soon she was to be put to the test by her accession to the throne. The Crown, rescued by her father from the disrepute brought upon it by the abdication of Edward VIII, and the attendant circumstances of that event, was never more worthily bestowed than when it was entrusted to Her Majesty, Queen Elizabeth II.

The recalling of a minor incident in her second visit to our Assembly gives me pleasure still.

Security considerations had necessitated that admission to the Assembly Hall should be, on that occasion, strictly by ticket. But when the Receiving Party were taking up position just inside the West door, a sympathetic Assembly Officer came to see if, as Convener of the Business Committee, I could, even yet, do something for two elderly ladies who had come a long distance to see the Queen but who had not applied for admission cards. What made matters worse for them was that the crowd around the East door, by which the Royal Party were to enter, was so dense that the two ladies, handicapped like Zacchaeus by lowness of stature, had very little chance of catching even a fleeting glimpse of the Queen. Could I do anything at all for them?

I had an idea. Admission to the Hall was impossible, and nothing could be done for them at the West door. I urged them to go as quickly as they could to the other door and take up positions as near as they could to that door. The Royal Party were to leave by that exit — a fact of which the general public were not as yet aware.

They lost no more time; and when the press photographs appeared next morning there they were — almost within touching distance of the Queen as she lingered to say her farewells to the officials of the Assembly who had accompanied her and her party to their cars. The broad smiles on their faces were eloquent of their delight. They had not only seen the Queen; they had actually been photographed with her!

Royal visits are rare occurrences, but seldom an Assembly passes without bringing distinguished persons, other than the Sovereign's representatives, to its platform. One of these, in 1918, was David Lloyd George, then at the height of his fame and with unblotted escutcheon. He visited all three Assemblies — Church of Scotland, United Free Church of Scotland and Free Church of Scotland, and, in a letter subsequently written to Sir William Robertson Nicoll, he was openly critical in his comparisons. The Church of Scotland he passed over lightly and briefly. In the United Free Church Assembly he found an assumption of superiority — "an indefinable air of implying, 'We are the people of Scotland. If you please us, you have done all that is necessary.' He was glad to get out and go to the Wee Frees, and he had not been there for five minutes before he felt he was at home."

The Free Church Moderator that year was Rev. (afterwards Dr.) Donald Munro, of Ferintosh, and Lloyd George judged his speech "the best of the three Moderators...Sometimes hesitating for a word, but always getting the right word in the end."

Still recalling his visit, he added, "I tell you Nicoll, these people are conserving something that ought to be conserved, whatever it be."

"His whole heart went out to them." says Robertson Nicoll, "and he made there by far the best of his Edinburgh speeches."

There were other visitors to the Assembly from time to time who formed the same impression of what the Free Church was conserving, who, happily, were less vague about its identity and character. One of these, Mowat Phillips, a well-known journalist who wrote an article for *The Daily Mail* on our 1949 Assembly, was generous — perhaps even to a fault — in his tribute.

"With much justice on its side," he writes, "the Free Church of Scotland can claim to be the direct lineal descendant of the Reformation in Scotland — in the senior line. .... The Free Church, with its uncompromising austerity in outlook, may not command much numerical support, but no Scotsman with a sense of history can deny it respect."

I have often regretted, however, that the Free Church, in recent times, has not been more diligent in making its distinctive testimony more widely known. In this connection, I recall my last conversation with Principal J.K. Cameron — a conversation, indeed, that was terminated by the sudden heart-stroke that took him away from his earthly labours later that day.

Recalling the events of the Church's post-1900 struggle he remarked, "You know, I sometimes wonder if our success in the House of Lords Appeal was altogether an unmixed blessing for us. I have never doubted, of course, that we did the right thing in resisting the excommunication with which the United Free Church attempted to serve us. We had not departed from the original testimony and Constitution of the Free Church of Scotland, so we refused to be disinherited. The material inheritance went with the spiritual, as the Lord Chancellor so cogently argued, and we succeeded in preserving a Reformed heritage for Scotland in 1900, just as the Disruption Fathers did in 1843."

"Our mistake was," continued Dr. Cameron, "that we rested too long on our laurels. True, we had come through a gruelling time, and were tired. But it is a significant fact that during the period when we had to fight for our very existence, and were forced to explain ourselves to the people of Scotland at meetings held here and there all over the country, the stricken Free Church continued to recover and regain strength. And then we eased off; we rested too soon and too long, and the work suffered in consequence."

Those, I gathered, were the lines that Principal Kennedy Cameron had intended to follow in his College Opening lecture. But it was never delivered, and the College missed the recall to action that its veteran Principal had intended to sound. Scottish inter-Church relations have become less strained in recent years, and that is all to the good. But the policy that expresses itself in the slogan "Let's forget the things wherein we differ and concentrate on those wherein we agree" will not get us far along the road to real unity. For many of the things that divide us are of vital importance and simply must not be treated as trivial.

One of our Assembly visitors from overseas whose visit gave me immense pleasure was the Australian preacher and writer Dr. Frank W. Boreham. His popularity at the time was such that Professor Daniel Lamont, who introduced him to the Church of Scotland

Assembly, could hardly be charged with overfulsomeness when he described him as "the man whose name is on all our lips, whose books are on all our shelves, and whose illustrations are in all our sermons."

In the Free Church his most ardent admirers were unquestionably Rev. Duncan MacDonald of Milton, Glasgow, and Professor Alexander Ross of the Free Church College. It was to Duncan MacDonald that the duty was assigned of expressing the Assembly's thanks to our visitor, mainly because (as Dr. Alexander Stewart pawkily remarked) Mr. MacDonald was reputed to have, not just one bee but two, in his bonnet — Bunyan and Boreham! Rising to the Moderator's call, Duncan immediately admitted his addiction, adding defensively, "And where else, Moderator, could you find such busy bees and such rich honey?" It was not, however, that his doctrine fathomed the depths of theological thought; far otherwise. Indeed, the criticism most frequently levelled against him was that his books were simple to the point of triviality. But the general public did not think so, and volume after volume came from his tireless pen in steady succession.

Boreham met a real need in this connection. The value of a good book lies largely in its readability, and Boreham always excelled in that virtue. He solved for many of us the problem of how to get a good book into the hands of a religion-shy reader with some hope of its being read. The recipient of the book is not really drawn to it, but for the sake of the donor he feels that he must know what it is all about. Soon he is reading for the sheer charm of it. There were times indeed when he did seem to have over-run his hand, and to be ready to lay aside his over-wrought pen, and then, unexpectedly, another volume with all the old sparkle would appear. Frank Boreham did not plumb the depths of philosophical speculation and theological investigation, but his friend and biographer, T. Howard Crago, apostrophises him fittingly where he writes:

"*Vale* F.W. Boreham. The world is poorer for your passing, but richer for the legacy you left it — the lovely lines, the sweetening influence — and the signposts pointing to the Saviour."

18: That They May Be One

The war years had suspended international Church gatherings, but with the ending of hostilities the *'get-together'* movement was resumed. It was felt that the Christian world ought to be more closely integrated, and that the question of Church and State relations ought again to be examined. Soviet Russia had brought the Church to the point of extinction. Nazi Germany had cast evangelical church leaders into concentration camps because of their voiced opposition to the programme of the party and with the philosophy underlying it. The Church in Norway had suffered at the hands of the German invaders because of the stand they had made for the faith of their fathers and the political implications of that faith. Dutch churchmen had languished in the darkness of *Dachau* for their resistance to the indoctrination of their school-children with the Nazi philosophy. The time was ripe for a reappraisal of Church and State relations.

Along with this, the Ecumenical Movement was gathering momentum in the post-war world, and seemed prepared to go to any lengths in doctrinal adaptation and compromise to achieve its stated aim. But there were questions which had to be asked and answered.

So far as the the Roman Catholic Church was concerned, the reunion of the Church was simple. The Church of Rome was Apostolic and Infallible, and therefore authoritarian. The Reformed Church, like the Prodigal Son, had left the Father's House, but his door was always open for their return.

All would be forgiven and forgotten if they came back and accepted anew, and with penitence, the parental rule which they had formerly rejected. The Papacy changed its voice. Protestants, who used to be stigmatised as *"heretics"*, were now referred to as *"separated brethren"*. But the change of voice did not signify a change of heart. Rome is not really interested in the modern Ecumenical Movement, nor in its projected World Church. She herself is the World Church and is ready to receive the "separated brethren" who have lost their way. She has abjured the language of threatening and is experimenting with words of enticement, like Mary Howitt's spider:

Will you walk into my parlour? said a spider to a fly;
'Tis the prettiest little parlour that ever you did spy.

And the Liberals in the various Protestant denominations are distinctly interested. Christian unity, they tell us, is what our Lord prayed for. And they quote His words, *"That they all may be one."* But they stop quoting too soon, for the next few words make it quite clear that the unity which Christ desires is unity of a quite specific character; *"as Thou, Father, art in me, and I in Thee, that they also may be one in us...".* That is to say, a spiritual unity, attained and maintained by sanctification through the Truth.

Clearly then, the makeshifts and compromises of Liberal ecumenism make no real contribution to Christian unity. The World Council of Churches presented an impressive facade, but its unity was not strength. Malcolm Muggeridge in an impish review of their Uppsala meetings said that they reminded him of a sight that he used frequently to see on Friday nights from a window in his lodgings in student days. There was a pub along the street where a group of men used to meet for a drink on the evening of pay-day. But, invariably, they tarried too long at their cups, with the result that at closing time they were very tipsy. There was a show of unity, a great display of *bonhomie* as they lurched unsteadily and with linked arms along the street. But the inter-twined arms were not symbolical of brotherly affection; they had become a necessity of the situation. United they stood (but only just!); divided they fell! The symbolism, in its application to the World Council, was not without point.

The Reformed Churches, however, were beginning to feel that more was required of them than that they should stand apart from a spurious ecumenism, and in 1945 a group of Reformed Churches, representing the Netherlands, Southern Africa and the United States of America, met in Grand Rapids to discuss the possibility of setting up a truly Reformed body which should find its bond of union and basis of Christian co-operation in the Word of God and the Reformed Confessions. The hidden and essential spiritual unity of the true Church ought to be given open and definite expression in an age of doctrinal confusion. The media for the accomplishing of this purpose lay ready to our hand in the historic Reformed Confessions.

The idea caught on, and it was resolved to initiate a body which was ultimately designated the Reformed Ecumenical Synod, and appointed to meet in Amsterdam in August 1949.

The Free Church of Scotland became associated with the R.E.S. from that time, and, as Moderator of the General Assembly that

year, I was appointed to attend the Amsterdam meetings, as were
also Rev. Alexander Macdonald M.A., the Retiring Moderator, and
Professor David McKenzie M.A., from the Free Church College.
We went via Paris to make some Reformed contacts there. My
friend of College days, Rev. Donald Caskie D.D., who was then
minister of the Scots Kirk in Paris, made arrangements for us. He
himself was on holiday in Islay at the time, but he kindly obtained
reservations for us at a comfortable little hostelry — the *Hotel
Avenida*, just off the *Champs Elysees*.

It added interest to our stay in Paris that this hotel was one of
Donald's underground contacts in his *Tartan Pimpernel* days when
he put his very life in danger in the interests of many of his fellow-
countrymen, and others, whom he helped back to freedom after
their escape from Nazi-occupied territories. Many of these escapees
had reason to remember the *Hotel Avenida* with gratitude. An
accomplished lady who had been part of the underground
organisation was still in charge.

Our principal places of interest in Paris were those associated with
the Protestant movement — particularly with the Massacre of St.
Bartholomew, when the streets of the city ran with martyr-blood,
and the bells of *Notre Dame* Cathedral rang out the Pope's
jubilation over the foul event. The adjacent memorials of the
atrocities of the French Revolution also stirred our thoughts by their
ghastly memorials of lawless times, and we seemed to hear the
pained voice that once had spoken from Olivet in rebuke of
Jerusalem's crowning sin, speaking in like terms to modern Paris;
"...*if thou hadst known, even thou, in this thy day, the things which
belong unto thy peace — but now they are hid from thine eyes*..."

And, even yet, Paris is not listening.

But a visit to the College of the Reformed Church in the city
served to remind us that the influence of the faithful remnant is not
yet spent.

Continuing our journey via Brussels, there was much, even in the
names of the places through which we passed, to remind us of the
appalling holocausts of the two World Wars; indeed, the black
embers of the second of these could be said to be still smouldering.

The Reformed Ecumenical Synod met under the hospitable and
efficient sponsorship of the *Gereformeerde Kerken* of the
Netherlands. A plaque on the wall of the *Kaisersgraacht Kerk*,
where the introductory meeting was held, was a reminder of
Holland's recent sufferings at the hands of her Nazi oppressors.
Some radio equipment had been discovered under a floor in the

building, and the Church Officer had been charged with operating it. On interrogation, he confessed to being in the underground movement, but declared that the pastor knew nothing about it. They nevertheless went to the minister's house and, late on the Sabbath evening though it was, demanded that he come with them immediately.

The elderly minister had gone to bed, tired and unwell after the exertions of the day, but they laid him under arrest and took him to his Church where they confronted him with the discovery they had made, and with the Church Officer who was already in their hands. The pastor protested his complete ignorance of what had been going on, and his innocence of any participation in it. The Church Officer upheld his pastor's testimony and reaffirmed that he himself, and he alone, knew of the existence of the radio equipment that had been brought to light.

But it was to no avail. There and then, without any semblance of trial, both men were shot dead. It was a sombre introduction to the work which had brought us together.

Our meeting in the *Kaisersgraacht Kerk* was truly international and Reformed. As was fitting, it was led by the host Church, with Professor G. C. Berkouwer, of the Free University, presiding. The addresses were given by Professor Bouma, of Grand Rapids, U.S.A.; Professor Jooste, from Potchefstroom University, South Africa; and myself. The fact that my address was the only one given in English — except for the chairman's remarks — gave Professor Berkouwer an idea that caused me some embarrassment. Acting upon the spur of the moment, he announced that, before calling the next speaker — Professor Jooste — he was going to give an impromptu resume of my address in Dutch, for the sake of the non-English speaking people who were listening to the addresses on the radio in their own homes — this without prior warning to the radio representatives present!

I looked with dismay at Professor Jooste, who was sitting beside me, and whispered my apology for the encroachment on his time but he was his usual gracious self in the matter. When the meeting was over and I asked one of the officials how much of the meeting they had been able to put across, he looked at me with surprise and exclaimed, "How much? Why, all of it." "But," I replied, "we were running around thirty minutes late."

I do not know in words the Dutch equivalent of *So what?* but I got the message when it was transmitted to me in a glance, especially when the verbal explanation was added — "Our Dutch listeners would raise an outcry if we were to cut short a religious programme like this. In any case, the next item has already been given a new placing."

When the Synod proper began its sittings the following morning Professor G.C. Aalders of the Free University was cordially elected Moderator. His gracious personality made an impact for good upon the whole Synod. He had been seized by the Gestapo as a hostage in reprisal for an incident with which he had had no connection, and had been held in prison under threat of the death penalty merely in retaliation for an action with which he was not even charged.

The host church had seen to it, in drawing up the programme, that within the time-limits available, opportunity would be taken to show us as much of their interesting country as possible. A day was given to a memorable tour of North Holland. We visited the fertile *polders*, reclaimed from the North Sea and transformed into excellent farmlands. Many of these, however, had been devastated by the routed German armies as they were driven back in 1945 by the allied troops. The work of repairing the breached dykes and of rebuilding the ruined townships was already far advanced for, as in the days of Nehemiah, *"the people had a mind to work"*.

We broke our journey at the farming township of *Middlemeer*, the fishing port of *Volendam*, the cheese-market town of *Alkmaer* and the fascinating little *Isle of Marken*, which has since been joined to the mainland by a causeway. The Church there had prepared an excellent tea for us, served by the young women of the congregation in their attractive native costumes. The elders could have been from the Western Isles of Scotland — men of solid character, well versed in theology as a result of their delight in the study of Holy Scripture.

The Town Council of Amsterdam also rose to the occasion by holding a civic reception for us, and treating us to a delightful tour of Amsterdam's famous canals and harbours. The *Burgomaster*, a Huguenot by descent, greeted us with a most telling speech of welcome which suggested that the blood of his Reforming ancestors still ran strongly in his veins.

The discussions at the sessions of the Synod were exhilarating and promising and the Reports subsequently published held out good prospect of consolidated and co-ordinated witness and effort by the Churches represented.

A visit to the Free University, founded largely by Holland's famous theologian and Prime Minister, Dr. Abraham Kuyper, was an interesting event of the closing days of the Synod. It was conducted by Professor Aalders who had been a student under

Dr. Kuyper. It was a pleasure to meet again Miss Catherine Kuyper whom I had met in Edinburgh in 1938 at the meeting of the last Calvinistic Congress. She had been a secretary to her father during his time as Prime Minister and her reminiscences of those stirring times in both Church and State made interesting hearing. Holland's debt to Abraham Kuyper has never been fully reckoned and indeed, at the present time, is in danger of being forgotten.

We finished our meetings in Amsterdam with a feeling of having made a promising beginning. At the outset we had bound ourselves to a Reformed Constitution, broadly and unambiguously based upon the historic Creeds and Confessions to which we were pledged in our respective denominations. Membership of the World Council of Churches was to be regarded as incompatible with membership of the Reformed Ecumenical Synod. A difficulty arose here from the fact that some of the Eastern Churches desiring membership of the Reformed Ecumenical Synod were already in the World Council of Churches and were anxious to be in membership of both. The Synod, from the outset, took its stand against dual membership. Nothing was done precipitately, however, and Standing Committees were appointed to give fuller consideration to the important questions which had been before the Synod.

The next full meeting of Synod was appointed to be held in Edinburgh in 1953, with the Free Church of Scotland as host. I was appointed Convener of the Preparations Committee and no Chairman could ever wish for a more enthusiastic body of helpers.

High tribute was duly paid to Edinburgh Town Council for the readiness with which they co-operated with us. Their reply to my letter intimating our forthcoming meetings was immediate and cordial. They would lay on a civic reception for our guests and would we have time for a tour of the city and its environs as well? They would be glad to lay on a fleet of coaches for the purpose. We looked at our programme again and saw to it that the needed time was made available, to the great enjoyment of our visitors.

We ourselves, as host church, arranged a tour through the Trossachs, fitting it in with a cruise on Loch Katrine. The weather conditions could not have been better and the constantly changing beauty of the landscape was breath-taking.

The B.B.C. also showed their interest in the Synod, not only by giving helpful reports of the meetings, but also by providing facilities for a Sabbath evening broadcast from the Edinburgh studios of the Corporation. Again, the service was made as representative as possible. As Moderator of Synod I was appointed to preside, but the sermon was preached by Rev. W. J. Grier B.A. of Belfast and Professor Ned B. Stonehouse of the Orthodox Presbyterian Church of America also took part.

We were courteously received and welcomed by Dr. Melville Dinwiddie, head of the B.B.C. Religious Broadcasting Department in Scotland who, incidentally, was surprised when I told him of the historic link that we of the Free Church of Scotland had with the place where we were met. It was the location of the old Queen Street Hall where the continuing Free Church had held its first General Assembly after its exclusion from the Free Church Assembly Hall at the formation of the United Free Church after the Church Union of 1900. Such are the currents and cross-currents of ecclesiastical history!

Dr Dinwiddie was interested to hear that I had two photographs of the Assembly hanging in my room in the Free Church Offices and a few days later he called in to see them. They had belonged to Dr. Donald Maclean and been given to me by his widow.

The next meeting of the R.E.S, was held in Potchefstroom, Southern Africa in 1958. Hearing that, as chairman of the Interim Committee, I was likely to be one of the Free Church delegates to the Synod, our missionaries in the Southern African field asked the Foreign Missions Committee to convey to me their desire that I should make myself available for visits to our Missions for such time as I might find possible.

I found that I could fall in with their plan, though in terms of weeks rather than months, so I readily agreed, and assured them that I would not shy at a heavy programme.

They took me at my word.

Air-travel to Southern Africa had not fully caught on by 1958, and in my case, my preference would always be for surface-travel if time-limits allowed. Along with that, my wife was to accompany me on this visit, and, as she was recovering from an illness at the time, our doctor strongly advised the more leisurely mode of travel. Accordingly, we booked for East London by the Union Castle liner *Stirling Castle*.

The journey was a sheer delight. The day at Madeira was full of interest; and I regretted that our stay was not longer, for I should have liked, if possible, to trace the footsteps of Dr. Robert Kalley — the pioneer Free Church missionary to the island, and afterwards to Brazil.

The islanders came on to the ship with their wares, and wits were pitted against wits as the battle of salesmanship proceeded. But the sight that drew the crowds was that of the children, little more than babes many of them, diving off the ship into the sea in pursuit of the coins that the passengers tossed into the water for them. In the brilliant sunshine one could see the glinting coin in the clear water slithering its way to the bottom with the child unerringly in pursuit. And seldom indeed did one resurface without the coin between its lips. As a display of skill it was fascinating, but as an instance of exploitation of little children, and a revolting exhibition of heartless commercialism, it could hardly be surpassed. Some of the parents literally tossed these youngsters overboard with their own hands to send them on their way.

An unexpected pleasure awaited us on our first evening in Capetown. A message awaited us requesting us to phone a certain telephone number from which an unidentified caller had been trying to make contact with us. When I phoned the number given, my caller turned out to be Mrs. Dewar, the widow of our pioneer missionary, Rev. Alexander Dewar, who took the leading part in reorganising the Free Church Mission in Southern Africa after the Church Union of 1900. Mrs. Dewar and her son, Ian, were now resident in Capetown, where Ian held an important legal appointment. They had heard that we were on the *Stirling Castle* and immediately tried to make contact with us so as to invite us to their home. A better introduction to Southern Africa could not have been planned for us. Ian's car, driven by his devoted native chauffeur, was at our disposal all next day to take us to places which, without such a provision, we could not have visited.

But to speak of *Odey* as Ian's *chauffeur* would be to give a very inadequate impression of the relations between them. Ian had been early stricken with an illness which had largely incapacitated him for life, and *Odey* was his personal attendant — indeed, one might say, his *alter ego*. I have never seen such complete devotion to a master as was shown by *Odey*. He did practically everything for him, and seemed able to anticipate his every desire and need. The *rapport* between master and servant was complete.

The rounding of the Cape of Good Hope, on the last leg of our voyage to Port Elizabeth, was a real test of our sea-worthiness. The Bay of Biscay had been nothing by comparison. The Cape is indeed a place where *"deep calleth unto deep"* as the Indian Ocean meets the Atlantic; and he is a brave man who can round the Cape in a storm without gastronomic upset!

But that was not what made our arrival at Port Elizabeth such a welcome event. Rather it was that we were met by Rev. Joseph and

Mrs. Helen McCracken, whose friendship we had enjoyed for many years, and who were to be our hosts for the first week of our visit to the mission-field in which they were labouring.

No time was to be lost. We arrived on a Saturday forenoon and were off at 8 o'clock the following morning for our first service. It was to be held up country at Patentie, and in most primitive circumstances, for this was a new area. Our place of worship was a native school — as primitive a seat of learning as could be found anywhere, and as a place of worship more rudimentary still.

It was a lovely morning, and we revelled in the wide vistas of the African *veldt*. A lone ostrich looked at us enquiringly, obviously regarding our presence as an unwarrantable intrusion, but, deeming discretion the better part of valour, it took off with a turn of speed that intimated the end of the brief encounter!

We arrived at our meeting-place well ahead of our congregation, for punctuality does not rank highly among the local people, so we sat patiently in the genial warmth of the morning sunshine until the sound of distant singing broke the almost eerie silence.

"There they are coming," said Mrs. McCracken. "That is their song of witness to the non-Christians around them. They want them to know that their religion is one of *joy* — joy in the Lord."

Louder and louder became the singing, and as the singers drew nearer we could see how the rhythmic swaying of their bodies responded to the cadences of their song of witness. Their pleasure at meeting us was registered in their smiles of welcome.

Then followed the most primitive communion service I have ever seen. The building where we were assembled owed nothing to architectural planning. The walls were of clay and wattle. The seats, hard and backless, were occupied for the most part by women and their babies. The men squatted on their heels at the walls. The communion vessels matched the rest of the furnishings in crudity. But seldom have I been so awesomely aware of the Lord's Presence as I was among those simple people. And how they sang! Harmony seems to come naturally to them, and you felt that you simply *must* join in.

The sacrament of the Lord's Supper was followed by some baptisms, and to my astonishment, I heard my own name given to a little baby boy and my wife's to a little girl. The choice of names, we were told, was meant as a token of respect to the visitors.

The service was rounded off by a short prayer-meeting, shared by the office-bearers. One dapper little man became quite emotional as he led in prayer, and had to break off for a moment or two in order to regain his composure. There was a murmur of sympathy from the congregation, and somebody struck up the 23rd Psalm in *Xhosa*, and to a haunting *Xhosa* tune. The rest of the congregation joined in. It was a moving interlude, after which the elder resumed his prayer.

I asked an interpreter afterwards what the elder had been praying about when he became so overcome, and he replied that he had been thanking God for sending them the Gospel of salvation, and for the Free Church, who had been the means of its transmission. With a full heart he had been invoking God's blessing upon all the Church's activities, and praying that she might always be kept in the faith that had come to mean so much to others.

I found the incident deeply impressive. This was a new angle on things. We always expect that Christians in the home Church should be much in prayer for the young Church in the Mission field, but to find that the Lord was giving the Mission Churches a similar prayer-concern for the parent Church was surely evidence that the Apostolic injunction was bearing fruit, *"Bear ye one another's burdens, and so fulfil the law of Christ."*

Our time in the Free Church Mission area was fairly evenly divided between districts then superintended by Rev. J. McCracken, Dr. J. Campbell Andrews and Rev. Huite Sliep. It was a rare privilege to be their guests during those weeks, and to see something of their work. One felt a throb of real life in it all, and the enthusiasm with which their extension work was being prosecuted was encouraging. The church-building activities made their own appeal even to the numbers of heathen who came along not only to see what was happening but also to lend a hand with the work, and learn from the missionaries what it was all about.

The fact that the Reformed Ecumenical Synod was meeting in Southern Africa on that occasion meant that it was accessible to all our missionaries in that region, and our fellowship with them was thereby prolonged. Our conversations were stimulating and helpful and had the effect of bringing Reformed Missions into closer co-operation than had previously been the case.

The R.E.S. held its 1958 session in Potchefstroom, as the guests of the *Gereformeerde Kerken* of Southern Africa – otherwise known as the *"Dopper Kerk"*. They are descendants of the *Voortrekkers* — the pioneers — who had moved northwards from the old Dutch settlements in the Cape. The impressive Voortrekker Monument near Pretoria is a magnificent memorial of a heroic enterprise, and it richly repays a visit. The name *Potchefstroom* is a compound one. The *trekkers* leader was a man "Potgeiter", so they used the first syllable of his name as the first syllable also of the place-name. Potgeiter served them as leader, or *"chef"*, so the second syllable in the place-name denotes his office; while the third syllable in the place-name describes the nature of their place of settlement. It was by a stream, or *stroom*. So there you have it. His name was *POTgeiter*; his office was that of *CHEF*, or leader; and he led them to a place whose most important feature for a settlement was a *STROOM*, or a stream.

Potgeiter and his associates chose wisely, and Potchefstroom over the years has developed into an attractive and industrious community. Strong Calvinists themselves, they took steps to ensure that their children should be brought up in the Reformed Faith, not only in Church but in the school. So they kept both institutions in the closest relation with each other. They founded a theological seminary where their rising ministry were equipped for their high calling; and then expanded the theological school into a University which has grown in a most extraordinary way.

Later, I again visited Potchefstroom to take part in the Centennial celebrations of the University and, incidentally, to deepen my acquaintance with the scholarly men to whom the maintenance of this rich Christian heritage has fallen.

The "success story"of Potchefstroom University is one that will bear comparison with anything of a similar character that appears in the annals of the Reformed Church in any country. The spiritual interests of the students were safe-guarded from the very beginning by the measures taken to ensure that the teaching in all the faculties as they developed was in harmony with Christian standards and principles. The motto chosen, IN U LIG (a quotation from Psalm 36:9), expresses both the faith and aim of the founders, and reveals the source of their success.

It was my privilege on one occasion to preach in the Church of Potchefstroom which is, perhaps, the one most closely related to the University, and it was a joy to see so many of the staff from the different faculties joining in the worship and work of God's House and supporting the cause of the evangelical faith. It was good to meet again Dr. V.E. d'Assonville, now Professor of Church History in the Theological Faculty. He had put in a year's study in Edinburgh while preparing his thesis on *John Knox and the Institutes of Calvin*, and had made St. Columba's his spiritual home. In the Foreword to his thesis, which was later published, he graciously acknowledges the help of Dr. A.M. Renwick in his researches. Contacts of this kind, between Reformed scholars — even when language problems arise — are of great value, and ought to be maintained and extended.

But my "home from home" in Potchefstroom was, most of all, the hospitable residence of Dr. W. Robbertse, who was then Dean of Faculty of Science. Professor and Mrs. Robbertse have a perfect genius for friendship and their talented family take after them. It is the home in Potchefstroom with which we have had our most frequent contacts, and where our fellowship has always been spiritually enriching.

Professor E.P. Groeneveldt was elected Moderator of the Potchefstroom R.E.S. and his administration was marked by wisdom, shrewdness and patience. As events proved, these qualities were all needed.

The Report which gave the Synod its liveliest moments was undoubtedly that on Race Relations. The mis-representations of Father Trevor Huddleston in his widely-read book, *Naught for your Comfort*, had much to do with this development. Huddleston propounds the view that apartheid in Southern Africa is the outgrowth of the Reformed Churches there. Calvinists in Africa, he avers, regarding themselves as God's elect people, consider themselves as a master-race, entitled for all time to hold in subjection the accursed sons of Ham. But as well as revealing his misconception of Calvinism, Huddleston here attributes to the Calvinism of Dutch South Africans an attitude that has grown up rather with their Nationalism. Theology and politics, it is true, tend to become bewilderingly interwoven in Southern Africa, but in the *Report on Race Relations* submitted to the Synod, the fact was noted that "the South African member Churches are constructively critical of government policies, and are truly concerned with the Christianisation and development of the non-white races."

The Report further comments, "the fact that in Adam all human beings are equally subject to sin, and *'come short of the glory of God'* (Romans 3:23) implies that, in its relationship with God, no single race may deem itself entitled to a privileged position and consider itself superior to other races."

A reply to Huddleston's book was published by Alexander Steward under the title *You are Wrong Father Huddleston*. I had read *Naught for Your Comfort* before going to Southern Africa, and I very much wanted to obtain a copy of Steward's reply. But all my efforts met with failure. Huddleston's book was available almost everywhere, but Steward's book was nowhere to be found.

Some booksellers "hadn't heard of it." Others opined that I would have "great difficulty in obtaining a copy in this country." And one man, as if affronted by my request, replied bluntly, "No, I decided not to stock it."

Not until I reached Potchefstroom was I able to obtain a copy. And when subsequently, by the kindness of Professor du Plessis, whose life had been devoted to the deepest interests of the *Bantu* people, I was able to spend a day in Sophiatown, and other places mentioned by Father Huddleston, I came away with a lowered estimate of both his judgment and reliability. Marxists are adepts at fishing in troubled waters and unfortunately their hooks are being baited by some professing Christians whose philosophy is the flat negation of their religious profession.

The infiltrations of Communism are greatly facilitated by such people. At Fort Hare University, for example, I was shown specimens of pernicious leaflets which had found their way, nobody knew how, into the classrooms. And, on another occasion, during a visit to the splendid new University of the North, one of the native Professors told me of the constant trouble they were having with mischief-makers who were unceasing in their efforts to turn the students against the University authorities. And the situation generally is certainly not helped by the stiff intransigence of the Nationalists in Parliament.

One of our asides while at the Synod was a visit to a gold mine. We descended by one shaft and ascended by another which was almost two miles distant. We made the journey underground by a narrow-gauge railway in open wooden-seated carriages which jolted and swayed all the way through the long, narrow tunnel which connected the two shafts, to the accompaniment of an ear-splitting, clattering noise that put me off gold-mines for ever! Our kind hosts provided us with glasses of ice-cold tomato juice at the end of the journey. But mine was never finished! And I have never had one since!

We were told by a tongue-in-cheek official at the beginning of our visit that free samples of the mine's product were not given, and that stern measures would be taken with any visitor who might endeavour surreptitiously to possess himself of one, however small it might be! But some time after, one of our American friends had the misfortune to slip into some sludge in a dimly-lit passage, greatly to the detriment of his lower garments. Helping hands were immediately at his service, and he was taken away to have his trousers seen to while we awaited his return and plied our guide with questions about the gold industry in general.

In an incredibly short time our American friend was back with us, thoroughly cleaned up and looking little the worse of his mishap, except for a still noticeable dampness in his trousers, which was very quickly dealt with by the warm African sunshine when we returned to the surface. Amid uproarious laughter, our American brother was congratulated on his ingenuity in devising a means of obtaining specimens of the mine products, and over the failure of the ruse!

From Potchefstroom we went to Umtata with Rev. and Mrs. Huite Sliep, and were their guests for the few remaining days of our stay in South Africa, visiting as much as possible of the wide area under their care. The communion service at Mgokolweni was a fitting climax to what had been a most interesting sequence of varied engagements. And there had been some surprising encounters also. For instance, in Potchefstroom I was introduced to a young man whom I had baptised, at the request of his parents, in St. Columba's, Edinburgh, during the war years. They were stationed in Great Britain during that period.

Then, there was my meeting with Professor Zass, of Fort Hare University, who told me of a visit that he had paid to Scotland a year or two before, and of a quite remarkable man whose acquaintance he had made on a long train journey in Scotland. He was sorry that he could not recall his name, but he remembered that he was a Professor in Edinburgh; he thought, of Church History. He was such a genial man, so eager to make the journey interesting to his fellow-traveller; such a mine of information about the places they were passing through; and such a zealous Calvinist. "But what was his name? If I could only remember his name," he said, "perhaps you would know him."

"From your description of him," I said, "I think I can tell you his name. Was it Renwick?"

"That's the very name," cried Dr. Zass, "Do you know him?"

When I told him that Dr. Renwick was one of my elders, Professor Zass was delighted, and charged me to convey to him his warmest regards, which I duly did.

In Umtata, on another occasion, Mr. Sliep took me to see Mr. MacKenzie, the Presbyterian minister there. Mr. MacKenzie had asked Mr. Sliep if he thought it would be possible to have me preach in his Church at one of the services on my last Sabbath in Umtata. Mr. Sliep was able to tell him that my time was fully booked for that day, but promised to take me along to see him for a few minutes the following day if possible.

When we did call it was Mr. MacKenzie himself who received us, and when his wife came in later and greeted me her accent moved me to reply in Gaelic, *"Cha chreid mi nach 'eil Gaidhlig air an teangaidh sin?"* (I believe there is Gaelic on that tongue). She replied with astonishment, *"Tha gu cinnteach; ach ciamar 'tha Gaidhlig aig fear de 'ur 'n ainm-sa?"* (There is indeed; but how comes it that a man of your name has Gaelic?).

For the next few moments Mr. MacKenzie and Mr. Sliep lost us!

It turned out that Mrs. MacKenzie was from the Island of Lewis, and that, during her student days in Aberdeen, she used to worship in the Free Church there which was then under the ministry of my friend and former fellow-student, Rev. Duncan Leitch M.A., for whom she had, very understandably, the highest regard.

But of all my casual contacts in Southern Africa quite the strangest in many aspects was my encounter with a Mr. Donald Macleod hailing from Lochaber.

It happened on this wise.

At the opening and, more or less, informal meeting of the Reformed Ecumenical Synod in Potchefstroom I had been one of the speakers and had said some things that the press and radio (presumably in a news famine!) had judged worth recording. The sequel was that, two or three days later, I had a letter from this Mr. Macleod. He had heard the references to me on the radio, and they had set him wondering if I was the person who had written the biography of his brother, Principal John Macleod D.D.. He had not picked up my name very clearly on his radio. His newspaper, the following morning, however, in its report from the Synod, had confirmed his tentative identification. And now he was writing to ask if there was any way by which we could meet while I was in Africa.

As it happened, we had planned to spend a night in Durban on our way to Umtata, and would be passing through his home-town. We promised to look him up. But as we left Durban on the day appointed, and I looked for his letter I found, to my dismay, that I had mislaid it and had no note of his address.

My first thought was to call at a Post Office and see if they could help us. As soon then as we entered the town we began to look for one. Somebody spotted what looked like one on the other side of the street, and I got out to enquire. As I waited a moment to cross the street I came up to an elderly gentleman who was standing there, it would seem, for the same purpose. Acting upon a sudden impulse, I decided to seek his help.

"Excuse me, sir," I began. . . but I got no farther along that line;

for the man who looked up at the sound of my voice was the very image of Dr. John Macleod. "Pardon me," I stammered, "are you, by any chance, Mr. Donald Macleod?" "I am," he beamed. "And you'll be Mr. Collins."

We accompanied him to his lovely home, overlooking the beautiful shore of the Indian Ocean, and situated in a veritable Garden of Eden, yielding all manner of fruits.

Not even between twin brothers have I ever seen a closer likeness than I did between Donald and John Macleod. It entered into their very speech — the same quick utterance, the same soft accents, even the same gestures and mannerisms.

Donald Macleod had trained as a lawyer, and in that capacity had served one of the gold-mining companies for many years. We had much to talk about, but too little time to cover it all.

We had spent two thrilling days in the Kruger National Park on our way back from Potchefstroom. I have never taken kindly to the idea of holding wild beasts in captivity for the sake of gaping visitors. Better surely to let the wild beasts live their natural lives, and encage the visitors for the period of their visit, the duration of which is in accordance with their own choice; to encage *themselves* rather than sentence those fine animals to life imprisonment for the pleasure of the visitors, whose safety is well provided for! Regulations for visitors are strictly imposed. They must not at any point leave their cars, except at certain points of interest where armed men are on guard or, of course, within the stockades encircling the huts where they were to spend the night. The dangers are jocosely exaggerated on some of the picture post-cards which are sold in the shops within the stockades, one of which depicted a lioness and her cubs surrounding a car full of frightened passengers. The cubs are hungry, and are biting their way through the body of the car while mother-lion looks on approvingly saying, "Keep on, my dears. I know the shell is hard, but the kernel is very sweet!"

An eerie silence descends upon the landscape at night, broken only by the raucous croaking of the outsize frogs in the nearby Skukusa river.

We breakfasted early, for we wanted to visit a nearby water-hole when the animals would be gathering there to drink. It was a beautiful sight in the cool of the morning. As we resumed our journey we caught up with what visitors to the Reserve want most to see – a pride of lions. We were warned never to dispute the right of way with the wild animals and, indeed, we had no desire to do so. We valued every moment of their company. On they plodded, with every indication of having had a hearty breakfast, and showing no desire as yet to supplement it. The morning sunshine seemed to invite a quiet rest. After a mile, or so, they left the road to ourselves and veered off to the left, probably to some quiet resting-place whose comfort they had already sampled.

We came away with the feeling that the Reformed Ecumenical Movement was making gratifying progress. It was growing in numerical strength, and in understanding. The Reports submitted and discussed at its sessions revealed an increasing sense of purpose and vocation. Plans for a more efficient Secretariat were being followed out. On the whole the situation seemed very encouraging, and the delegates reported in that strain to the Churches which had sent them.

We thanked God and took courage.

19: Grand Rapids: 1963

The delegates who were appointed to the Grand Rapids Synod of 1963 looked forward to the event with great expectations. The R.E.S. was going back to its birth-place. The proposal that it had made to the Reformed Churches had won favour in many lands. It was not yet 17 years in existence, but already it comprised some 2.5 million members in the many lands from which it was drawn. The Christian Reformed Church was to be host on this occasion, and it had a reputation for doing things in a big way.

This time I expected to be less involved in Committee work than at former meetings, and thus to have more time for the cultivation of friendships formed in earlier days. But, alas,

> The best-laid schemes o' mice and men
> Gang aft agley.

At its first session I was again called to the Chair.

On previous occasions the Moderator had been chosen from one of the member churches in the country where the meetings were held, and nothing seemed more certain and appropriate than that the Moderator for the Grand Rapids Synod should come from one of the American constituent churches. But it was the unpredictable that happened, with the result that instead of the easier time I had been promising myself, I was launched into what must have been quite the heaviest programme of ecclesiastical duties that I have ever faced within the time limits set. Indeed, the fact that we finished within those limits was due in the main to the excellent co-operation and high competency of my associates on the Moderamen – Professor John Murray from Philadelphia; Professor Fred Klooster, from Grand Rapids; Professor Herman Ridderbos, from Kampen, Holland; and Dr. Paul Schrotenboer, then of Hamilton, Canada.

My first public duty was to reply to a cordial message of greeting from President John F. Kennedy, and, very soon thereafter, to send a message of sympathy to the President and Mrs. Kennedy on the death of their baby son.

The public meetings of the Synod attracted large audiences, and the delegates, drawn from twelve countries, gave heartening expression to the potential for spiritual growth and influence that exists where Christians bring their problems to the light of Holy Scripture, with sincere invocation of the Spirit's guidance.

The programme was an ambitious one, and did not confine itself to theological and ecclesiastical questions, but faced up to some of the burning issues of the day, in industry and commerce, in religion and morals, in race relations and public morals. The work-plan envisaged required an efficient secretariat, and, as a beginning, the Synod elected Dr. Paul Schrotenboer as its General Secretary.

The "*Moderamen*" (for we adopted a Dutch term, denoting the Moderator's Committee) worked long and strenuous hours, meeting early each morning to put the finishing touches to the programme of the day, and then late at night, after the evening session of Synod, to tie up the loose ends of the day's work. Between everything, the time for social fellowship had to be scaled down to a minimum. The times that I had promised myself for relaxation in the company of such old friends and veterans in the faith as R.B. Kuyper, Cornelius van Til, Martin Wyngaarden and John K. Kromminga had to be reduced to little more than passing greetings. In my confidence that I would not be one of the officers of Synod on this occasion, I had readily fallen in with the request of Rev. Murdo MacRitchie, our Free Church minister in Detroit, to preach there on the mid-Synod Sabbath, and again on my homeward journey the following week.

After the close of the Synod on the last Friday night the Moderamen had to sit on to deal with urgent business. Progress was slow and the business was intricate, and we were all tired. To add to our difficulties a violent thunderstorm broke out around midnight. Everything indicated the expediency of adjournment. Wearily, we decided to call it a day and meet again after early breakfast the next morning to finish our work. We eventually closed our meeting just in time to let me catch my plane to Detroit!

I was glad of the relaxation in the comfortable home of my kind host and hostess, Mr. and Mrs. Donald Macleod, and of the opportunity to preach again to Mr. MacRitchie's congregation. But Prestwick Airport was a welcome sight as we descended to its runways in the clearing light of the following Tuesday morning.

Had it all been worth while?

Even with the weariness of a gruelling fortnight still upon me I had no hesitation in affirming that it was. Christian unity is an end to be patiently and earnestly pursued, and it can be achieved only when we put ourselves under the teaching of God's Word, and the direction of the Holy Spirit. Subsequent events in the R.E.S. provided painful proof of that fact.

When it met again in Holland, in 1968, and under the Moderatorship of Professor Klaas Runia, then of Geelong, it was soon evident that a serious cleavage was building up in the Synod. The pro-World Council section of the membership were still resisting the Synod's sustained rejection of dual membership of constituent member-churches in both the R.E.S. and the W.C.C., but the Gereformeerde Kerken of the Netherlands were now making it clear that their course was set for membership in the W.C.C.. Along with that, there had been clear evidence of doctrinal laxity among certain of their Professors and Pastors, and, despite advice repeatedly given by the R.E.S. to the bodies concerned, very little attention was being paid to these directives. Reluctant to force the issue the Synod let the matter be remitted "for further consideration" to successive Synods until it became evident that a policy of attrition was being pursued.

The climax came when the General Synod of the Gereformeerde Kerken took a line which favoured a change of attitude to sex-perverts. It was proposed that not only full communicant membership in the Church be open to them, but even that there should be no bar to their admission to office.

Some of the R.E.S. constituent members - including the Free Church of Scotland — were quick to notify the Interim-Committee of the R.E.S. of their strong opposition, warning that, unless the Gereformeerde Kerken rescinded this decision, they be expelled from membership of the R.E.S..

The General Secretary of the R.E.S. and certain representatives of the Gereformeerde Kerken of the Netherlands came to Edinburgh to talk over the situation with certain members of the Free Church. We listened to them patiently as they urged us not to think of withdrawal at this stage, but we made quite clear that our advice to our own Committee would be to serve the R.E.S. with an ultimatum that unless they dealt firmly with the defaulting Church at the next meeting of the R.E.S., we should resign our membership.

It is now a matter of history that the R.E.S. did not take decisive action at that meeting, and that a number of member-churches withdrew from the Synod in consequence. But the spirit that motivated the formation of the Synod lives on, and the need for such a body still exists. The dissenting Churches have renewed contact with each other, and met in conference in Edinburgh in 1985. They have made known their willingness to rejoin the R.E.S.

if and when the Synod purges itself of the reproach of tolerating abominations that are condemned in every mention of them, both in the Old Testament and the New and, in every instance, punished with the utmost severity; abominations that, down the centuries, have brought Divine judgment upon mighty nations, and that, indeed, are working the destruction of our modern civilisation. The production of Christian unity is ultimately the work of the Holy Spirit and, on our side, it calls for prayer, patience and perseverance. There will still be set-backs and disappointments; but we shall learn by our mistakes, and be sustained by the thought that the endeavours of all who truly seek the prosperity of Zion shall be crowned with success in a promised time of revival when *"Thy watchmen shall lift up the voice; with the voice together shall they sing, for they shall see eye to eye when the Lord shall bring again Zion."*

20: Within Thy Gates, O Jerusalem

In 1965 I had a letter from the Church Travel Club which brought to fulfilment a dream which I had cherished for many years. The letter invited me to lead a party on a visit to Israel. I could not accept too soon.

As a school-boy I had read a series of articles by Rev. Andrew Burnett of Kilcalmonell Free Church, in which he told of a visit he had paid to the Holy Land. They ran for some months in *The Instructor*, and they held my keen interest from the first to last. And now, with complete unexpectedness, my longed-for opportunity had come.

We flew out from Gatwick on a cold night in April, and in the clearing dawn we were looking down over Cyprus, making for Damascus. There we stopped for an hour or two, and then took off again — this time for Amman.

It seemed as if, suddenly, history had gone into reverse. The last part of our flight was relatively short and we were flying at a lower altitude. The morning was now brilliantly clear and the visibility perfect. A ribbon of green vegetation betokened the presence of water, and, lo, a picture from Psalm 23 came alive. For there, just below, in our line of flight, appeared a white-clad figure, followed by a straggling line of sheep; the Eastern shepherd at the head of his flock, leading them slowly to new pastures at the beginning of the new day:

> *In pastures green he leadeth me*
> *The quiet waters by.*

Amman next! And here the ancient and modern appeared to be making a real effort to come to terms. A donkey carrying, precariously on its back, a washing machine! And this along the main thoroughfare of Jordan's capital! Jordanians — some in the picturesque garb of their fathers — and others in modern dress of the Western world co-mingling in business!

Incongruously, a fleet of American limousines were awaiting us at the airport, all with Jordanian drivers, ready to speed us on our way to Jerusalem and establish, it seemed, a new record in the process. If such an establishment as a "Jehu Motoring School" were conceivable, it would be easy to conclude that all Arabian drivers were trained there. Certainly, the Biblical description of Jehu's driving was applicable. Driving "furiously", yet with complete competency, they transported us over the Judean hills, and up the steep road from Jericho to Jerusalem at breakneck speed, and to the accompaniment of a ceaseless and discordant cacophony of motor-horns.

Jerusalem! The sight of the massive walls and girdling hills stirred up a flood of mingling emotions in the heart. Jerusalem! Chosen of God to be, in a special sense, His dwelling place in the land which by covenant He had of old given to His people. Jerusalem! The city of David and of David's greater Son. Jerusalem, where kings reigned and prophets ministered. Jerusalem that crowned its awesome catalogue of martyrdoms with the crucifixion of the Son of God. Jerusalem, where *"He was wounded for our transgressions and bore the chastisement of our peace;"* where He died that we might live. Jerusalem, where the Risen Christ gave His Church her marching orders and energised her by the Pentecostal unction. How these thoughts kept crowding in as we walked her streets! Jerusalem had much to show us; much more to suggest to us and teach us.

The question as to which of the reputed Calvarys, if either, is the true one did not matter so much after all. The garishness of the Church of the Holy Sepulchre did little to strengthen its claim to be the place of the Cross and the brief resting-place of His mutilated body before His triumphant Resurrection and ascension to the right hand of eternal majesty. The remarkable skull-formation of Gordon's Calvary and the quiet peace of the Garden Tomb nearby corresponded more closely to our preconceptions of these holy sites. But did it matter? The stirring and overpowering fact was that we were on the holiest spot in all the world; the place where the Lamb of God suffered, the just in the room of the unjust, and where the awesome rending of the Veil in the Temple signalled the ending of the old order and the beginning of the new. For there, *"by one offering He hath perfected for ever them that are sanctified."*

If, as has been aptly said, Israel is a commentary on the whole Bible, Jerusalem supremely is the place where the two Testaments meet. Take Christ as your clue to "all the Scriptures", as He Himself did in conversation with His disciples on the Emmaus Road, and through the clearing shadows of the Old Testament you will come to the shining realities of the New. For, as Dr. Stuart Holden so finely put it, "In the Old Testament all the lines of its teaching converge upon Him Who is to come. In the New all the lines of living light radiate from Him who has come. In the Old Testament He is prepared for. In the New He is proclaimed! In the Old Testament He is enfolded. In the New He is unfolded! In the Old Testament He is latent. In the New He is patent! In the Old Testament He is declared. In the New He is demonstrated!"

Yes, Jerusalem had much to offer us, and we were eager to receive. Israel is a small country, and when these tours are well-planned — as ours certainly was — it is quite astonishing how much can be packed into 14 or 15 days. We operated from two main bases, Jerusalem and Nazareth.

Our hotel in Jerusalem was entirely modern, situated just outside the city wall, and looking across to the Dome of the Rock, an unpleasant reminder that alongside the early Christian Church had arisen Mohammed and his fanatical following who had succeeded in well-nigh exterminating the Church over a wide area of its early conquests.

A pleasant surprise awaited us almost at the very moment of our arrival. There was a small bookshop near-by the hotel, and while we awaited the call to our afternoon meal, my close friend ever since student days, Rev. Alexander MacLeod of Nairn Free Church, walked across with me to see what it was offering for sale. And there, on a book-rack at the very door, was Professor A.M. Renwick's popular book *The Story of the Church*. How Dr. Renwick would have rejoiced to see it there! His *Story of the Church* on sale in the place where the incomparable STORY began! But my good predecessor in the Free Church College had been called from his earthly labours just a few months before. The book passed through several editions, each of which became an occasion of joy to the zealous author, not in any self-congratulatory sense but rather from his feeling of high privilege at having been commissioned to render this service to the Church of Christ.

Our hotel was situated just a short distance from the Garden of Gethsemane, a place for ever hallowed by the "strong crying and tears" of our Lord as He entered upon the final stages of His humiliation and sorrow as the "Suffering Servant" of whom Isaiah had spoken so long in advance of His advent. The rock which is pointed out as the precise location of His agony will appeal only to the credulous, and do nothing to inspire piety and strengthen faith; but to be in the Garden beyond the Brook Kedron, to which Jesus "oft-times resorted with His disciples", was an experience not to be missed.

In all, our tour extended to 17 days, and in a small country like

Israel much can be done in that time. Our local tours radiated out from two centres, Jerusalem in the south and Nazareth in the north. In the south we visited many places that made the Bible come alive. Hebron, for instance, with its cave of Machpelah, renowned as one of the cities of refuge, and as the place where David first set up his throne. Bethlehem, where Ruth the Moabitess had her home after she had come to set her trust under the wings of Israel's God and, more important still, where the Eternal Word was made flesh and came to dwell among men. Samaria brought its own cluster of thoughts. Inevitably, the conversation by the well of Jacob concerned the Living Water and the true worship. The ascent to the Samaritan synagogue on Mount Gerizim proved even more interesting than we had expected. The High Priest himself came to greet us and to show us the famous Samaritan Pentateuch.

The very place-names which marked our route that day proved a stimulus to memory and kept recalling us to the past. How, for instance, could we survey Bethel without thinking of Jacob and his encounter there with God? Could we visit Shiloh without recalling the boy Samuel who was there called to the leadership of his people or travel through Samaria without thinking of Ahab the king who *"sold himself to work evil in the sight of the Lord"* and who, with Jezebel his wife, took part in the murder of Naboth and many other atrocities?

A wicked place, this ancient stronghold; a place upon which the deserved judgments of God fell heavily. And yet a region specifically mentioned by our Lord when He gave His apostles their marching orders, "Ye shall be witnesses unto me, both in Jerusalem, and in all Judea, and in *Samaria...*". And when Philip went there with the Gospel and the Word took effect, *"There was great joy in that city."*

We were still based in Jerusalem when we made our excursion to the Dead Sea area. What a desolation it is! Yellow-brown hills rising sheer from the stony plain! The Dead Sea shimmering in the pitiless rays of the sun, with scarcely a scrap of vegetation to be seen anywhere. A weird, wild country which seemed to proclaim an ancient judgment of God; for we were now in the region of Sodom and Gomorrah. We extended our visit so as to devote some of our time to the area of the Qumran community and the nearby Caves where the Dead Sea Scrolls had been so strangely brought to light in 1947, and stood in the darkening shade of early evening, looking across the leaden waters to the distant hills of Moab. It would have met Cowper's longing for *a lodge in some vast wilderness*

but certainly not for the desiderated solace of

a boundless continuity of shade.

The intense eeriness of the whole region was positively awesome. And to think that it had once so resembled "the garden of the Lord" in respect of fertility, as to have lured away Lot from the holy fellowship of Abraham, and almost to have cost him his soul!

I was glad to have seen the place once. I should never want to see it again.

Our tour of Galilee had many special and obvious interests. We regarded ourselves to be privileged in being quartered in Nazareth during our stay in the North. Not that Nazareth is particularly interesting in itself. But for the fact that Jesus spent so much of His boyhood and early manhood there, it would have very little place on the tourist map. But it was good to live awhile where He lived, and familiarise ourselves with the sights that He saw, and to think of Him increasing in wisdom and stature, and in favour with God and men.

I recalled the words of David M. M'Intyre, "If we had gone to the Carpenter's shop, and watched the holy youth as He bent over the construction of some simple article of furniture, or fashioned some rude instrument of husbandry, and had asked Him, 'Son of Mary, what are you doing?', He might have answered, 'The will of God.' If we had drawn near to Him, as He instructed the ignorant, healed the sick, or opened the eyes of the blind, and had said, 'Prophet of Galilee, what are you doing?', He might have answered, 'The will of God.' If we had turned to Him as He hung upon the cross, bearing our sins in His own body, and had asked, 'Son of God, what art Thou doing?', He might still have answered, 'The will of God.' The will of God was the only thing that ever He did." (*Life in His Name.*)

And what a privilege to follow Him around in thought, as "He went about doing good", to Cana, where He made a social event among the common people the occasion of His first miracle; to Tiberias and the lakeside townships with which He was so familiar; to Capernaum where He made His home for a time; to Bethsaida, where he called his first disciples; and to Magdala, the home of Mary Magdalene.

Our intention had been to have a short service on the ship *Capernaum* which had been hired to transport us across the Sea of

Galilee from Tiberias to Gergasa, where the healing of the man with the Legion had taken place, but the Sea put up one of the sudden storms for which it is famous, and we had to retire below. But our compensation was that we saw it both in tempest and in calm in one and the same day.

It was Easter time when we made our tour of Israel, and over our first weekend there the Passover was being celebrated in the usual garish fashion and with very little more sense of reverence than one finds nowadays at an average Christmas party. Regretfully, the Church's Easter message seemed just as lacking in substance. Some of our party came to me to inquire as to the feasibility of having a short service of our own, and by the kindness of the hotel manager the facility was provided. We took the opportunity of reminding ourselves of how Isaiah, in the great 53rd chapter of his prophecy, foretold the advent of the Suffering Servant and the certainty of His success; basing our meditation on the words in the 10th verse of the chapter, *"Yet it pleased the Lord to bruise Him; He hath put Him to grief: when thou shalt make His soul an offering for sin, He shall see His seed, He shall prolong His days, and the pleasure of the Lord shall prosper in His hand."*

And therein Faith will find her guerdon.

He shall see the travail of His soul, and shall be satisfied.

On the evening before our party left Jerusalem for Nazareth, Alex MacLeod and I, while out for a walk, accidentally came upon the area where, at the time, the Gabbatha was being excavated after its long concealment, but was not yet open to the public. As a special favour, however, we were admitted and conducted through the part of the area that had been brought to light. It was the place where Pontius Pilate brought out Jesus to the mob and endeavoured to browbeat them into letting Him go. He tried *Compromise*; "I find Him innocent; you hold Him guilty. Come, I'll meet you half-way; I will scourge Him and let Him go." He tried *Politics*; "He is a Galilean, and Galilee is under Herod's supervision. Let Herod pronounce on Him." He tried *Subtlety*; "In observing the custom of choosing a prisoner for release at Passover time, I will limit their choice to Jesus and Barabbas and they will surely let Jesus go; Anyone rather than Barabbas!" He tried *Self-vindication*; "I will wash my hands of the whole incident. Look!" And the water tinkled into the basin. In the hands of Jesus water had turned into wine; in the hands of Pilate it changed into blood and the stain remained. And from the Gabbatha that voice seemed to follow us as we went on our way:-

What shall I do with Jesus which is called the Christ?

For Pontius Pilate's problem is our problem too. WE MUST DO SOMETHING WITH JESUS. Evasion of Him is impossible. We dismiss Him, but He comes back. Every time we hear His claims in the Gospel we are pressed for a verdict, and there is so much at stake! For "He that believeth on the Son hath everlasting life: and he that believeth not the Son shall not see life; but the wrath of God abideth on him."

What think ye of Christ? Everything depends on the answer.

> *Will you evade Him, as Pilate tried?*
> *Or will you choose Him whate'er betide?*
> *Vainly you struggle from Him to hide.*
> *What will you do with Jesus?*   *(A.B. Simpson)*

Gabbatha is a solemn place.

Epilogue

And now my pilgrimage is nearly over. Many of my fellow pilgrims have already finished their course. Like Bunyan's Mr. Standfast they have said:

"I have loved to hear my Lord spoken of; and wherever I have seen the print of His shoe in the earth, there I have coveted to set my foot too... for He has held me, yea my steps hath He strengthened in the way....." Their desire has been accomplished.

A final incident comes to mind in this connection. I was driving my elder, James Stewart, home after a Kirk Session meeting when he spoke of having been visiting in his district that day. He mentioned two gracious ladies of our acquaintance and then remarked, "Do you know what I was thinking as we spoke?" "I'd like to know," I replied. "I was thinking," said James, "if the Lord's people are so attractive in this life, what will they be like in the next?"

The question is not unanswered.

"Brethren, now are we the sons of God, and it doth not yet appear what we shall be; but we know that when He shall appear, we shall be like Him; for we shall see Him as He is."

.... And what more could heart desire?